ASIAN

ONE STEP AT A TIME

ASIAN

ONE STEP AT A TIME

THE ULTIMATE STEP-BY-STEP COOKBOOK

JODY VASSALLO

PHOTOGRAPHY BY CLIVE BOZZARD-HILL

❋ ❋ ❋

hamlyn

First published in France in 2007 under the title
Les basiques d'Asie, by Hachette Livre (Marabout)
Copyright © 2007 Hachette Livre (Marabout)

© Text Jody Vassallo
Photography by Clive Bozzard-Hill
Styling by Sonia Lucano

An Hachette UK Company
www.hachette.co.uk

First published in Great Britain in 2009 by
Hamlyn, a division of Octopus Publishing Group Ltd
2–4 Heron Quays, London E14 4JP
www.octopusbooks.co.uk

Copyright © English edition
Octopus Publishing Group Ltd 2009

ISBN 978-0-600-61951-2

A CIP catalogue record for this book is available from the
British Library

Printed and bound in Singapore

10 9 8 7 6 5 4 3 2 1

Measurements Metric and imperial measurements
have been given in all recipes. Use one set of
measurements only and not a mixture of both.
Standard level spoon measurements are used in
all recipes.
1 tablespoon = one 15 ml spoon
1 teaspoon = one 5 ml spoon

Nuts This book includes dishes made with nuts and
nut derivatives. It is advisable for those with known
allergic reactions to nuts and nut derivatives and
those who may be potentially vulnerable to these
allergies, such as pregnant and nursing mothers,
invalids, the elderly, babies and children, to avoid
dishes made with nuts and nut oils. It is also advisable
to check the labels of preprepared ingredients for
the possible inclusion of nut derivatives.

Eggs should be large unless otherwise stated. The
Department of Health advises that eggs should not
be consumed raw. This book contains dishes made
with raw or lightly cooked eggs. It is advisable for
more vulnerable people, such as pregnant and nursing mothers, invalids, the elderly, babies and young
children, to avoid uncooked or lightly cooked dishes
made with eggs. Once prepared these dishes should
be kept refrigerated and used promptly.

Milk should be full fat unless otherwise stated.

Butter is unsalted unless otherwise stated.

Fresh herbs should be used unless otherwise stated.
If unavailable use dried herbs as an alternative but
halve the quantities stated.

Ovens should be preheated to the specific
temperature – if using a fan-assisted oven, follow
manufacturer's instructions for adjusting the time
and the temperature.

INTRODUCTION

When I think of quick and easy delicious meals I'm immediately drawn to Asian cuisine. Most recipes only call for a wok or pan, and if you have purchased a rice cooker then you just need to push a button to cook your rice. The ingredients, I know, can sometimes be a little tricky to locate, but these days increasing numbers of supermarkets are stocking a wide range of Asian ingredients.

The most important thing to remember about cooking the recipes in this book is to get everything chopped and ready before you turn on the heat; this is because many stir-fries take less than 10 minutes to cook.

So pick a cuisine – Thai, Japanese, Vietnamese, Chinese or Indonesian – and select a recipe, follow the step-by-step photographs and see for yourself just how easy the dishes from these countries are to prepare. Before you know it you will have a repertoire that will rival your local takeaway.

✿ ✿ ✿

CONTENTS

1
STARTERS

2
MEAT

3
POULTRY

4
SEAFOOD

5
VEGETABLES

6
DESSERTS

APPENDICES
GLOSSARY • MENUS • TABLE OF CONTENTS • RECIPE INDEX
GENERAL INDEX • ACKNOWLEDGEMENTS

SEASONING A WOK

➵ **PREPARATION: 5 MINUTES • COOKING: 20 MINUTES** ➵

NOTE: Each time you use the wok, make sure you
wash it only in hot water – do not use soap.
Dry over a high heat and brush lightly with oil.

1	Wash the brand new wok in soapy water, scrubbing away any machine oil. Rinse under cold running water and dry.	2	Brush the entire surface with groundnut oil.
3	Put the wok over a high heat and heat until blackened. Leave to cool.	4	Mop up the excess oil with kitchen paper. Repeat the brushing, blackening, cooling and mopping about 3 times until the wok darkens.

HOW TO COOK RICE

❋ MAKES 875 G (1 LB 12 OZ) • PREPARATION: 5 MINUTES • COOKING: 15 MINUTES ❋

250 g (8 oz) jasmine or white rice

1	Rinse the rice under cold running water until the water runs clear.	2	Put the rice in a large saucepan, cover with cold water and bring to the boil.
3	Cook until tunnels form in the rice. Reduce the heat to low and cover the rice.	4	Leave to stand until all the liquid has been absorbed. Gently separate the grains with a fork.

SEASONED SUSHI RICE

❖ **MAKES 875 G (1 LB 12 OZ)** • PREPARATION: 5 MINUTES + 1 HOUR DRAINING • COOKING: 20 MINUTES ❖

325 g (11 oz) sushi rice

DRESSING:
2 tablespoons rice vinegar
1 tablespoon caster sugar
2 teaspoons salt

1 2
3 4

1	Wash the rice then drain for 1 hour. Put the rice in a pan, add 375 ml (13 fl oz) water and bring to the boil. Boil for 5 minutes.	2	Reduce the heat if you are using gas, otherwise take off the heat. Cover and cook or leave for 10 minutes until the liquid has been absorbed.
3	Heat all the dressing ingredients in a pan until the sugar has dissolved. Spread the rice out on a large tray, pour over the dressing and mix in.	4	Cover with a damp tea towel and leave to cool completely. Sushi rice only keeps for 1 day. Use in sushi rolls, chirashi sushi and temaki sushi.

STARTERS

SOUPS

SNACKS

APPETIZERS

TOM YUM GOONG

⇝ SERVES 4 • PREPARATION: 20 MINUTES • COOKING: 15 MINUTES ⇜

8 large raw prawns
4 garlic cloves, crushed
3 lemongrass stalks, sliced

200 g (7 oz) button mushrooms, halved
2 ripe tomatoes, cut into wedges
3 small red chillies, halved

5 kaffir lime leaves
3 tablespoons fish sauce
2 tablespoons lime juice, to serve

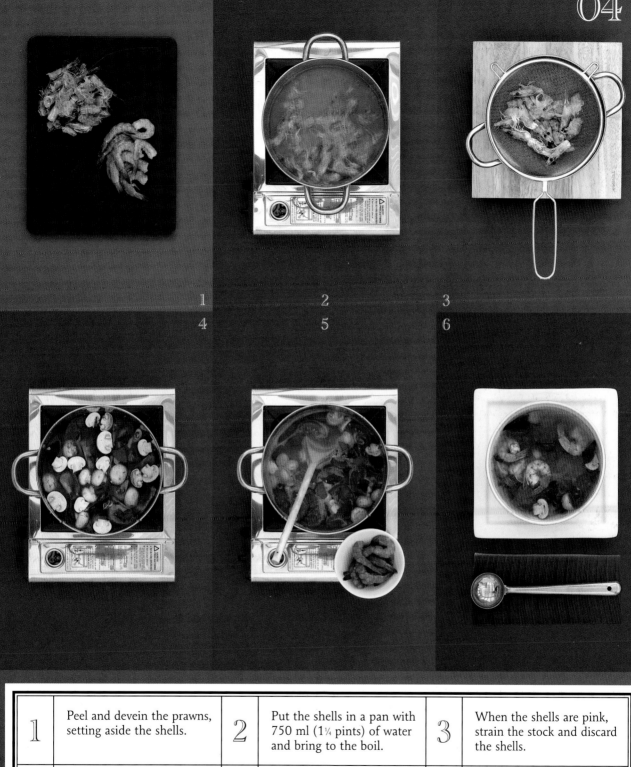

1	Peel and devein the prawns, setting aside the shells.	2	Put the shells in a pan with 750 ml (1¼ pints) of water and bring to the boil.	3	When the shells are pink, strain the stock and discard the shells.
4	Add remaining ingredients, bring to the boil, then simmer for 5 minutes.	5	Add the prawns and cook for 3 minutes. Remove from the heat.	6	Stir in the lime juice and serve at once.

TOM KAI GAI

❧ SERVES 4 • PREPARATION: 10 MINUTES • COOKING: 10 MINUTES ❧

5-cm (2-in) piece fresh galangal
2 lemongrass stalks, sliced
800 ml (1½ pints) coconut milk

3 small red chillies, halved
4 kaffir lime leaves, torn
300 g (10 oz) chicken breast, thinly sliced

2 tablespoons fish sauce
2 tablespoons lime juice
2 tablespoons fresh coriander leaves
(optional)

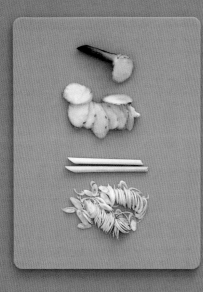

1 2
3 4

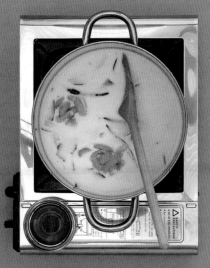

1	Cut the galangal and lemongrass into thin slices.	2	Put the coconut milk in a pan, add the galangal, lemongrass, chillies and lime leaves and simmer for 5 minutes.
3	Add the chicken and fish sauce and cook for 5 minutes, or until the chicken is tender.	4	Remove from the heat and stir in the lime juice and coriander, if using.

CHICKEN & CORN SOUP

⇥ SERVES 4–6 • PREPARATION: 5–8 MINUTES • COOKING: 5 MINUTES ⇤

3 corn cobs
2 x 425 g (14 oz) tins creamed sweetcorn
300 g (10 oz) chicken breast, diced

1 litre (1¾ pints) chicken stock
3 eggs
125 ml (4 fl oz) evaporated milk

sea salt
½ teaspoon white pepper
2 spring onions, finely sliced

1	Remove the corn from the cobs.	2	Bring the corns, chicken and stock to the boil, then lower the heat to a simmer.	3	Whisk the eggs in a bowl.
4	Gently stir in the eggs, allowing them to form thin threads. Cook for 1 minute.	5	Add the evaporated milk and season with salt and white pepper.	6	Sprinkle with spring onions before serving.

MISO SOUP

❧ SERVES 4 • PREPARATION: 10 MINUTES + 10 MINUTES SOAKING • COOKING: 10 MINUTES ❧

100 g (3½ oz) silken tofu
1 tablespoon wakame (seaweed)
1 teaspoon dashi granules

3 tablespoons red miso (shiro miso)
2 spring onions, finely sliced

1	Cut the tofu into small cubes with a sharp knife.	2	Soak the wakame in cold water for 10 minutes, then drain well.	3	Cook the dashi and wakame in 1 litre (1¾ pints) boiling water for 10 minutes.
4	Blend the miso with a little of the hot stock and return to the pan; do not boil.	5	Divide the tofu among 4 serving bowls.	6	Pour over the hot stock and garnish with spring onions. Serve immediately.

PHO BO

⟫ SERVES 4–6 • PREPARATION: 20 MINUTES • COOKING: 1 HOUR ⟪

1.5 litres (2½ pints) beef stock
50 g (2 oz) fresh ginger, sliced
2 onions, halved
2 cinnamon sticks
2 star anise

3 cloves
1 teaspoon black peppercorns
3 tablespoons fish sauce
625 g (1¼ lb) fresh rice noodles
100 g (3½ oz) bean sprouts

225 g (7 oz) beef fillet, very thinly sliced
2 spring onions, sliced
2 tablespoons fresh coriander
lime wedges and finely cracked black
pepper, to serve

1	Bring the stock, ginger, onions, spices, pepper-corns and fish sauce to the boil, then lower the heat and cook, covered, for 30 minutes.	2	Strain and discard the seasonings, then return the stock to the pan and bring back to the boil.
3	Put the noodles, bean sprouts and sliced beef into serving bowls.	4	Ladle over the stock, top with spring onions and coriander and serve with lime wedges and cracked black pepper.

GOI CUON

⇒ MAKES 8 • PREPARATION: 30 MINUTES • COOKING: NIL ⇐

75 g (3 oz) dried rice vermicelli
8 rice paper rounds, 22 cm (8½ in) diameter
20 g (¾ oz) finely shredded lettuce

16 fresh mint leaves
16 cooked prawns, peeled and deveined

DIPPING SAUCE:
2 tablespoons fish sauce
1 tablespoon lime juice
2 tablespoons sweet chilli sauce

1	Put the vermicelli in a bowl and cover with boiling water. Leave for 5 minutes.	2	Rinse and drain well.	3	Soak one rice paper round in cold water until soft.	
4	Put on a tea towel, then top with a good tablespoon each of vermicelli, lettuce and mint and roll over.	5	Top with 2 prawns.	6	Fold in the sides and roll up to enclose the filling.	➤

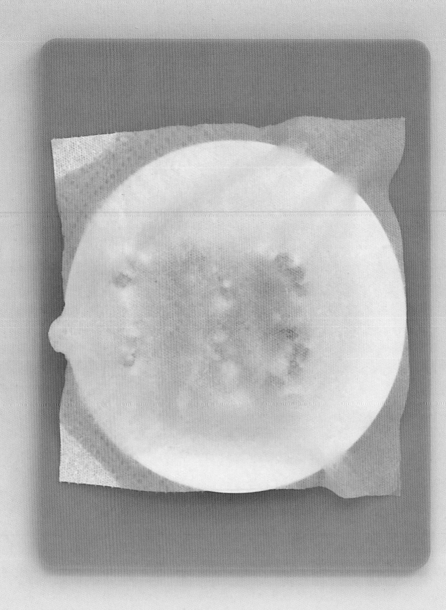

	Place on a plate and cover with damp kitchen paper while you prepare the remaining rolls.	**VEGETARIAN ALTERNATIVE** ❖ Use sliced firm tofu instead of the prawns.
7		

8 | For the dipping sauce, put all the ingredients in a bowl and mix to combine. Serve with the rolls.

SERVING SUGGESTION
✳
These rolls are also delicious served with a hoisin sauce topped with chopped peanuts.

NEMS

❋ MAKES 8 • PREPARATION: 30 MINUTES • COOKING: 20 MINUTES ❋

75 g (3 oz) dried mung bean vermicelli
6 dried shiitake mushrooms
1 carrot, finely grated
150 g (5 oz) minced pork
1 tablespoon chopped fresh coriander

8 rice paper rounds, 22-cm (8½-in) diameter
groundnut oil, for deep-frying
shredded Chinese cabbage, to serve
DIPPING SAUCE:
1 tablespoon fish sauce

3 tablespoons lime juice
1 clove garlic, chopped
1 small red chilli, seeded and chopped
1 teaspoon caster sugar

1	Put the noodles in a bowl, cover with boiling water and leave for 5 minutes. Rinse and drain, then cut into shorter lengths using scissors.	2	Soak the mushrooms in boiling water for 10 minutes, or until soft. Drain, then remove and discard the stalks. Finely chop the caps.
3	Put the noodles, mushrooms, carrot, pork and coriander in a bowl and mix well to combine.	4	Soak 1 rice paper round in cold water until soft. ➤

5	Place on a clean tea towel. Put 2 heaped table-spoons of the noodle mixture on top.	6	Fold in the sides and roll up to enclose the filling. Repeat with the remaining rice paper and filling.
7	Heat the oil and deep-fry the rolls in batches until crisp and golden. Drain on kitchen paper.	8	To make the dipping sauce, put all the ingredients in a bowl and mix to combine.

9   Arrange the rolls on a bed of shredded cabbage and serve with the dipping sauce.

VARIATION

❋

Substitute minced chicken for the pork.

SERVING SUGGESTION

❋

These rolls are delicious sliced into 3 pieces and served on top of noodles. (See Bo Bun recipe 28 and replace the beef with the sliced nems.)

DIM SUM

❖ MAKES 14 • PREPARATION: 40 MINUTES • COOKING: 15 MINUTES ❖

250 g (8 oz) minced pork
50 g (2 oz) chopped canned water chestnuts
1 tablespoon light soy sauce

1 tablespoon Shaoxing rice wine
½ teaspoon sesame oil
1 spring onion, sliced
1 tablespoon grated fresh ginger

14 wonton wrappers (square)
choice of dipping sauce, to serve

1 2
3 4

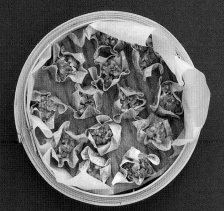

1	Put the pork, chestnuts, soy sauce, rice wine, sesame oil, spring onion and ginger into a bowl and mix to combine.	2	Put a tablespoon of the filling into the centre of a wonton wrapper. Gather up the edges to enclose the sides of the filling, leaving the top open. Repeat with the remaining wrappers.
3	Put the wontons in a steamer. Cover and cook over simmering water for 15 minutes.	4	Serve with your choice of dipping sauce.

EDAMAME

❖ **SERVES 4** • PREPARATION: 5 MINUTES • COOKING: 10 MINUTES ❖

500 g (1 lb) frozen soya beans in pods
2 tablespoons soy sauce
2 tablespoons rice vinegar
1 teaspoon grated fresh ginger

1 2
3 4

1	Cook the soya beans in a large pan of boiling water for 5 minutes, or until bright green and soft.	2	Rinse under cold running water and drain well.
3	For the dipping sauce, whisk the soy sauce, rice vinegar and ginger together.	4	Serve the soya beans in their pods with bowls of the sauce.

GYOZA

❧ MAKES 30 • PREPARATION: 30 MINUTES • COOKING: 15 MINUTES ❧

350 g (12 oz) minced pork
90 g (3 oz) shredded Chinese cabbage
2 spring onions, sliced
2 teaspoons grated fresh ginger
1 egg, lightly beaten

1 tablespoon soy sauce
2 teaspoons mirin
2 teaspoons sake
30 gyoza wrappers, or as needed
2 tablespoons vegetable oil

DIPPING SAUCE:
2 tablespoons soy sauce
2 tablespoons rice vinegar

1	Mix the pork, cabbage, spring onions, ginger, egg, soy sauce, mirin and sake together.	2	Lay gyoza wrappers on a board and put 2 teaspoons of the filling into the centre of each.	3	Brush the edges of the wrapper lightly with water.
4	Bring the edges together and pinch to seal. Repeat with the other wrappers.	5	Heat the oil in a pan and add enough gyoza to cover the base. Cook until crisp.	6	Add 125 ml (4 fl oz) water, cover and cook for 5 minutes. ➤

7	For the dipping sauce, mix the soy sauce and rice vinegar together.

TIP
❊

Gyoza can be made ahead of time and frozen, uncooked, in an airtight container until ready to use.

VARIATION
❊

For something different, try steaming or deep-frying the gyoza.

8	Serve the gyoza warm with the dipping sauce.

SERVING SUGGESTION
❈

Gyoza are delicious added to noodle soups. Cook as per the recipe and then float them on the top of Japanese udon soups.

VARIATION
❈

Try adding some finely chopped vegetables to the mixture, such as shiitake mushrooms, grated carrot, grated daikon (white radish) or shredded spinach.

CALIFORNIA ROLLS

➹ **SERVES 4** • PREPARATION: 20 MINUTES • COOKING: 20 MINUTES ➹

4–6 sheets roasted nori (seaweed)
550 g (1 lb 2 oz) cooked seasoned sushi
rice (see recipe 03)

2 tablespoons Japanese mayonnaise
8 crabsticks
1 avocado, cut into thin strips

TO SERVE:
soy sauce
wasabi

1 2
3 4

1	Put one sheet of nori onto a bamboo mat.	2	Spread the rice over two-thirds of the mat.	
3	Squeeze a line of mayonnaise over the centre of the rice.	4	Top with the crabsticks and avocado.	➤

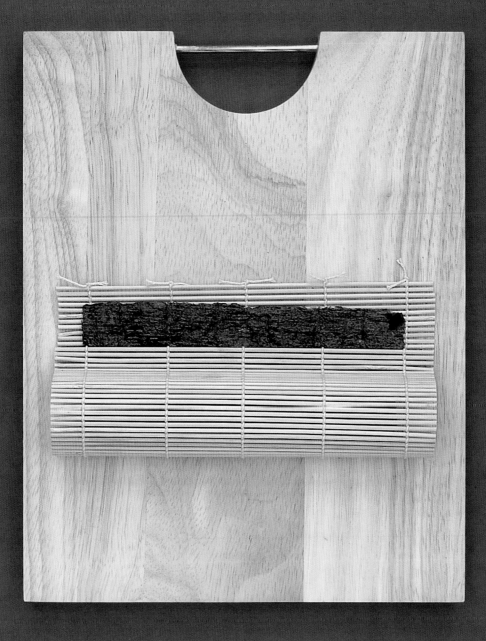

5	Roll up to enclose the filling, drawing the mat tight as you roll.

VARIATION
❋

Try substituting some sliced raw sushi-grade salmon or tuna for the crabsticks.

VARIATIONS
❋

Other ideas for sushi rolls include cooked teriyaki chicken, deep-fried vegetables, seaweed salad, pickled daikon (white radish) and finely shredded carrot, cucumber and tofu.

6	Using a sharp knife, cut the roll in half, then into thirds. Serve with soy sauce and wasabi.

TIP
❋

To keep any leftover nori sheets fresh, store them in an airtight container.

TIP
❋

Sushi rolls can be made ahead of time, but do not slice them until you are ready to serve.

FISH CAKES

➤ MAKES 24 • PREPARATION: 15 MINUTES • COOKING: 20 MINUTES ➤

500 g (1 lb) boneless white fish fillets, chopped
2 tablespoons red curry paste
1 egg
100 g (3½ oz) snake beans, thinly sliced

4 kaffir lime leaves, finely shredded
750 ml (1¼ pints) vegetable oil
DIPPING SAUCE:
1 small red chilli, chopped
¼ cucumber, finely chopped

1 tablespoon chopped fresh coriander
1 tablespoon white granulated sugar
125 ml (4 fl oz) white rice vinegar

1   2   3

4   5   6

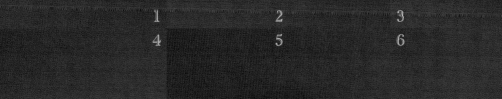

1	Put the fish, curry paste and egg into a food-processor and whiz until smooth.	2	Transfer the mixture to a bowl, add the snake beans and lime leaves and mix to combine.	3	Shape tablespoons of the mixture into flat patties.
4	Heat the oil in a wok and deep-fry the fish cakes in batches until golden. Drain.	5	For the dipping sauce, combine all of the ingredients in a bowl.	6	Serve the fish cakes with the dipping sauce.

PRAWN TOAST

⇝ MAKES 18 • PREPARATION: 15 MINUTES • COOKING: 20 MINUTES ⇜

10 slices white bread
750 g (1 lb 8 oz) raw tiger prawns, peeled
and deveined (equates to 350 g/12 oz
prawn meat)
2 teaspoons grated fresh ginger

1 egg white
2 teaspoons cornflour
2 teaspoons Shaoxing rice wine (optional)
2 tablespoons chopped fresh coriander
1 spring onion, sliced

4 tablespoons sesame seeds
groundnut oil, for deep-frying
sweet chilli sauce or soy sauce, to serve

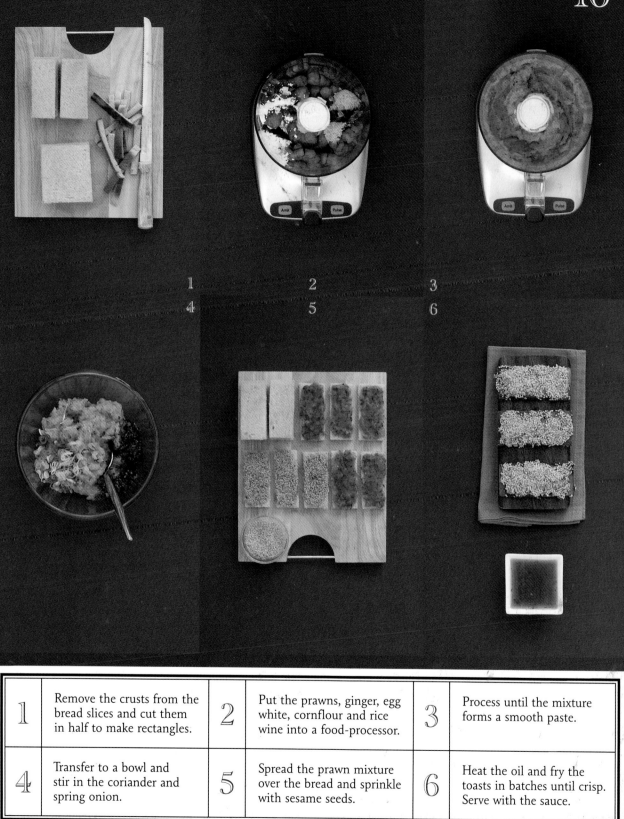

1	Remove the crusts from the bread slices and cut them in half to make rectangles.	2	Put the prawns, ginger, egg white, cornflour and rice wine into a food-processor.	3	Process until the mixture forms a smooth paste.
4	Transfer to a bowl and stir in the coriander and spring onion.	5	Spread the prawn mixture over the bread and sprinkle with sesame seeds.	6	Heat the oil and fry the toasts in batches until crisp. Serve with the sauce.

SASHIMI

➤ SERVES 4 • PREPARATION: 15 MINUTES • COOKING: 5 MINUTES ➤

200 g (7 oz) tuna
200 g (7 oz) salmon fillet
200 g (7 oz) fresh scallops

1 daikon (white radish), scrubbed
1 carrot
½ teaspoon wasabi

TOSA DIPPING SAUCE:
3 tablespoons mirin
75 ml (3 fl oz) soy sauce

1 2
3 4

1	Cut the tuna, salmon and scallops into 1-cm (½-in) thick slices.	2	For the dipping sauce, bring the mirin and soy sauce to the boil over a high heat for 5 minutes. Cool.
3	Using a mandolin or sharp knife, finely grate the daikon (white radish) and carrot.	4	Mound the vegetables onto the serving plate beside the fish and serve with the dipping sauce and wasabi.

CHICKEN SATAY

❖ **SERVES 4** • PREPARATION: 20 MINUTES + 15 MINUTES SOAKING • COOKING: 25 MINUTES ❖

500 g (1 lb) chicken breast fillet

SATAY SAUCE:
40 g (1¼ oz) peanuts
250 ml (8 fl oz) coconut milk

2 tablespoons red curry paste
1–2 tablespoons grated palm sugar
1 tablespoon tamarind concentrate (purée)

1	Soak several bamboo skewers for 15 minutes. Cut the chicken into cubes.	2	Thread the chicken onto the presoaked bamboo skewers.	3	For the sauce, dry-fry the peanuts, then crush them in a food-processor.
4	Heat the milk, add the nuts and remaining ingredients and cook for 15 minutes.	5	Barbecue or chargrill the chicken until tender, turning during cooking.	6	Serve the chicken with the satay sauce.

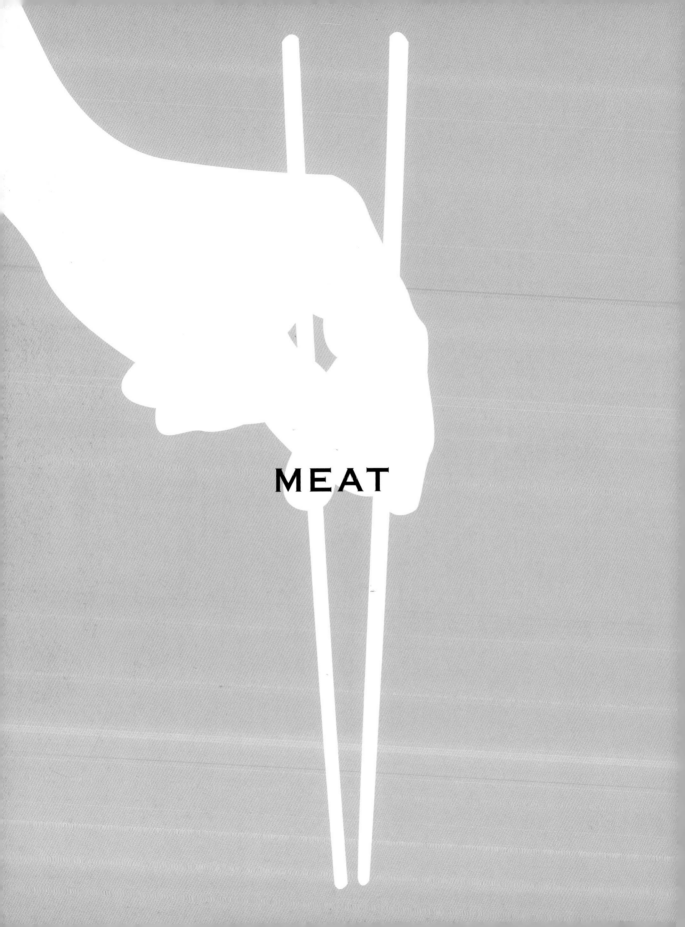

MEAT

STIR-FRIES

GRILLS & ROASTS

CLASSICS

CURRIES

LARB MOO

➤ **SERVES 4 • PREPARATION: 10 MINUTES • COOKING: 15 MINUTES** ➤

500 g (1 lb) minced pork
¼ teaspoon chilli powder
2 tablespoons chopped red shallots
or red onions

1 tablespoon finely chopped lemongrass
3 tablespoons fish sauce
3 tablespoons lime juice
2 tablespoons chopped fresh mint

2 tablespoons chopped fresh coriander
TO SERVE:
1 Little Gem lettuce, separated into leaves
lime wedges

1 2
3 4

1	Put the pork, chilli powder, shallots and lemongrass in a bowl and mix to combine.	2	Heat the wok over a high heat, add the pork mixture and stir-fry until the pork is cooked but not browned.
3	Turn off the heat and stir in the fish sauce, lime juice, mint and coriander.	4	Serve warm with lettuce and lime wedges.

SUNG CHOI BAU

❧ **SERVES 4** • PREPARATION: 20 MINUTES + 10 MINUTES STANDING • COOKING: 20 MINUTES ❧

1 iceberg lettuce
4 dried shiitake mushrooms
1 tablespoon groundnut oil
¼ teaspoon sesame oil

500 g (1 lb) fatty minced pork
2 garlic cloves, chopped
65 g (2¼ oz) tin water chestnuts, rinsed, drained and chopped

4 tablespoons oyster sauce
2 tablespoons Shaoxing rice wine
1 teaspoon caster sugar
2 spring onions, sliced

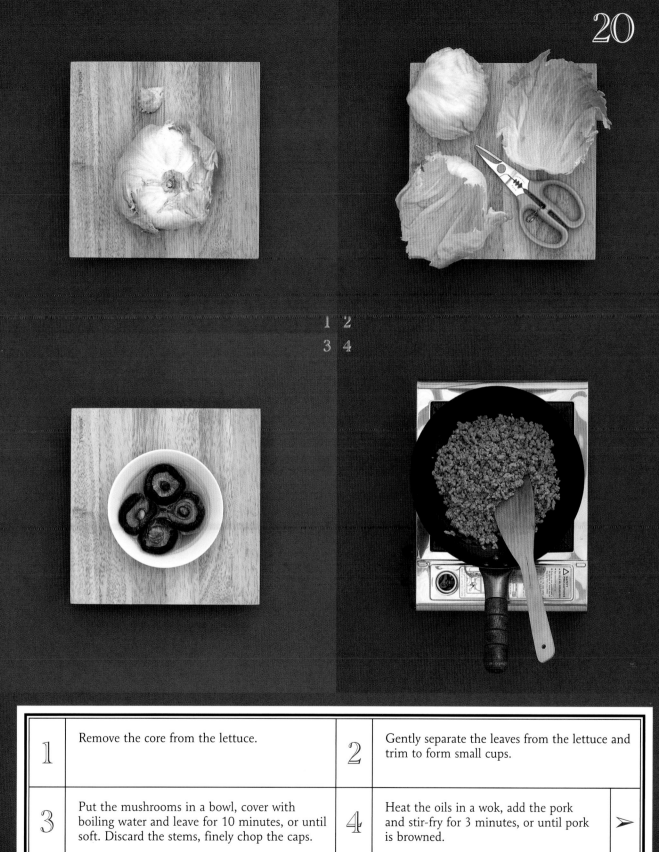

1	Remove the core from the lettuce.	2	Gently separate the leaves from the lettuce and trim to form small cups.	
3	Put the mushrooms in a bowl, cover with boiling water and leave for 10 minutes, or until soft. Discard the stems, finely chop the caps.	4	Heat the oils in a wok, add the pork and stir-fry for 3 minutes, or until pork is browned.	➤

| 5 | Add the garlic and water chestnuts and stir-fry for 3 minutes. Add the oyster sauce, rice wine, sugar and spring onions and bring to the boil. Cook over a high heat for 5 minutes, or until the sauce reduces slightly. | **VARIATION**
❉
Use minced beef or chicken instead of the pork.

TIP
❉
Try topping the sung choi bau with crispy fried egg noodles for some extra crunch. |

| 6 | Serve the meat in bowls with the lettuce leaves – allow each person to fill their own leaves with the meat filling. | **SERVING SUGGESTIONS**
❊
You can serve the sung choi bau either hot or cold. They are also good served as an appetizer at parties in baby cos leaves. |

BEEF IN BLACK BEAN SAUCE

❧ SERVES 4 • PREPARATION: 20 MINUTES + 30 MINUTES MARINATING • COOKING: 10 MINUTES ❧

500 g (1 lb) beef fillet, cut into thin strips
1 tablespoon light soy sauce
1 tablespoon Shaoxing rice wine
2 tablespoons groundnut oil
½ teaspoon sesame oil

1 onion, sliced
2 garlic cloves, sliced
1 red pepper, sliced
1 green pepper, sliced

4 tablespoons salted black beans, rinsed
and chopped
1 teaspoon caster sugar
4 tablespoons oyster sauce
freshly cooked rice, to serve

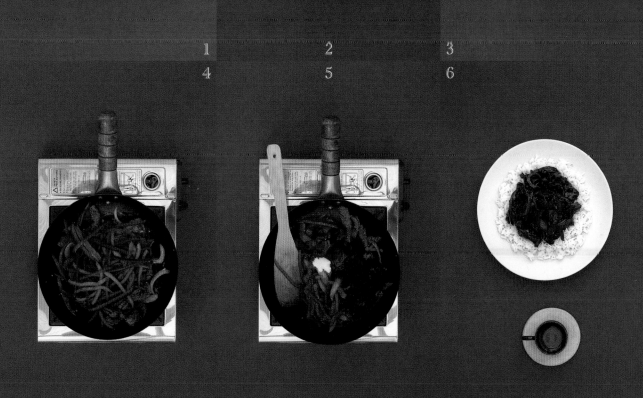

1	Mix the beef, soy sauce and rice wine together in a non-metallic bowl.	2	Heat the oils in a wok, add the onion and garlic and stir-fry for 3 minutes.	3	Add the beef and stir-fry for 5 minutes, or until the meat is tender.
4	Add the sliced red and green peppers.	5	Add the black beans, sugar and oyster sauce to the wok and stir-fry for 2 minutes.	6	Serve the beef with freshly cooked rice.

YAKI SOBA

SERVES 4 • PREPARATION: 15 MINUTES • COOKING: 15 MINUTES

1 tablespoon vegetable oil
300 g (10 oz) pork fillet, thinly sliced
400 g (13 oz) fresh hokkien noodles
200 g (7 oz) peeled cooked prawns

200 g (7 oz) Chinese cabbage, finely shredded
3 spring onions, sliced
1 red pepper, thinly sliced
3 tablespoons light soy sauce

1 tablespoon caster sugar
1 egg, lightly beaten
pickled ginger, to serve

| 1 | Heat 2 teaspoons of the oil in a pan, add the pork and cook until browned. | 2 | Cook the noodles in hot water for 3 minutes, then drain well. | 3 | Mix the pork, noodles, prawns, vegetables, soy sauce, sugar and egg. |
| 4 | Heat the remaining oil in a wok until it starts to smoke, then add the noodle mixture. | 5 | Stir-fry until everything is heated through and the egg is cooked. | 6 | Serve the noodles topped with pickled ginger. |

SHAKING BEEF

✈ **SERVES 4** • PREPARATION: 15 MINUTES + 30 MINUTES MARINATING • COOKING: 10 MINUTES ✈

5 Asian shallots
4 tablespoons white vinegar
1 tablespoon caster sugar
1 tablespoon fish sauce

4 garlic cloves, chopped
2 tablespoons vegetable oil
500 g (1 lb) rump steak, cut into small cubes

50 g (2 oz) butter
1 Little Gem lettuce, separated into leaves

1	Peel and thinly slice the shallots, put into the vinegar with 2 tablespoons of water and leave for 30 minutes.	2	Put the sugar, fish sauce, garlic, 1 tablespoon of oil and the steak into a bowl.
3	Heat the remaining oil and the butter in a wok over a high heat, add the beef and cook until browned but still pink in the centre.	4	Drain the shallots and divide among the lettuce leaves on a serving plate. Top with the cooked beef and serve.

CHAR SUI PORK

⇒ SERVES 4–6 • PREPARATION: 15 MINUTES + 2–8 HOURS MARINATING • COOKING: 30 MINUTES ⇐

2 garlic cloves, chopped
1 tablespoon grated fresh ginger
1 tablespoon malt vinegar
50 ml (2 fl oz) Shaoxing rice wine
50 ml (2 fl oz) hoisin sauce

50 ml (2 fl oz) Chinese barbecue sauce
1 tablespoon light soy sauce
500 g (1 lb) pork shoulder, cut into large pieces
1½ tablespoons honey

TO SERVE:
freshly cooked rice
steamed Asian greens, such as pak choi

1	Whisk the garlic, ginger, vinegar, rice wine, hoisin, barbecue sauce and soy sauce together in a bowl. Pour over the pork, then cover and chill for 2 hours, or overnight.	2	Preheat the oven to 240°C (475°F), Gas Mark 9. Arrange the pork pieces on a wire rack over a baking tray half-filled with water.
3	Bake for 30 minutes, basting several times with the marinade, until the pork is tender.	4	Put the honey in a pan and bring to the boil. ➢

		SERVING SUGGESTION
5	Brush the honey over the pork and set aside to cool.	The cooked sliced pork is delicious added to stir-fries with noodles and vegetables.

TIP
⁂

The longer you leave the pork in its marinade the more intense the flavour will be.

6	Slice the pork and serve with freshly cooked rice and Asian greens.	**SERVING SUGGESTION** ❀ Serve the sliced pork on top of wonton noodle soups.

TIP
❀

Use the cooked pork in rice paper rolls or sushi.

SESAME BEEF SALAD

❖ **SERVES 4** • PREPARATION: 10 MINUTES + 10 MINUTES RESTING • COOKING: 5 MINUTES ❖

500 g (1 lb) rump steak
1 tablespoon vegetable oil
150 g (5 oz) mizuna lettuce
3 spring onions
2 tablespoons sesame seeds, toasted

DRESSING:
3 tablespoons light soy sauce
3 tablespoons lemon juice
1 teaspoon caster sugar
1 garlic clove, chopped

½ teaspoon sesame oil
1 teaspoon grated fresh ginger

1	Whisk together all the ingredients for the dressing.	2	Rub both sides of the steak with the oil, then chargrill for 3 minutes on each side, or until cooked rare.	3	Loosely cover the steak with aluminium foil and rest for 10 minutes.
4	Cut the steak into thin slices with a sharp knife.	5	Arrange the mizuna lettuce, onions and steak on a plate.	6	Pour over the dressing and sprinkle with sesame seeds.

BUN CHA

❧ SERVES 4 • PREPARATION: 20 MINUTES + 4 HOURS MARINATING • COOKING: 20 MINUTES ❧

1 tablespoon grated palm sugar
2 tablespoons fish sauce
2 garlic cloves, chopped
2 Asian shallots, chopped
500 g (1 lb) minced pork
200 g (7 oz) dried rice noodles

DIPPING SAUCE:
4 tablespoons fish sauce
6 tablespoons lime juice
2 teaspoons caster sugar
2 red chillies, deseeded and finely
chopped

TO SERVE:
100 g (3½ oz) bean sprouts
fresh coriander and mint sprigs
lettuce leaves

1	Put the sugar and fish sauce into a small pan and stir over a low heat until the sugar melts. Cool.	2	Put the cooled sauce, garlic, shallots and pork into a bowl and mix to combine. Marinate for 4 hours.	3	Shape the mixture into patties. Use 2 tablespoons to make the shape.
4	Chargrill the patties until slightly charred and tender.	5	Mix the sauce ingredients. Cook the noodles in boiling water until soft. Drain.	6	Serve the patties on the noodles with the sauce, sprouts, herbs and lettuce.

BABI KETJAP

❖ **SERVES 4** • PREPARATION: 10 MINUTES + 30 MINUTES MARINATING • COOKING: 15 MINUTES ❖

500 g (1 lb) pork fillet
2 tablespoons plain flour
1 tablespoon soy sauce
½ teaspoon ground ginger

3 tablespoons vegetable oil
1 onion, finely chopped
3 garlic cloves, chopped
5 cm (2 in) piece fresh ginger, shredded

125 ml (4 fl oz) kecap manis
1 teaspoon chilli powder
1 tablespoon lemon juice
freshly cooked rice, to serve

1 2
3 4

1	Cut the pork into small cubes. Put the flour, soy sauce and ginger into a bowl and mix well. Mix in the pork and chill for 30 minutes.	2	Heat the oil in a wok, add the meat in batches and cook until browned.
3	Add the onion, garlic and fresh ginger and cook until soft.	4	Add the kecap manis, chilli and 3 tablespoons of water and cook for 5 minutes until thick. Stir in the lemon juice and serve with rice.

BO BUN

SERVES 4 • PREPARATION: 15 MINUTES + 30 MINUTES MARINATING • COOKING: 10 MINUTES

4 tablespoons fish sauce
3 tablespoons grated palm sugar
200 g (7 oz) thin dried vermicelli
2 tablespoons soy sauce
2 tablespoons oyster sauce

2 teaspoons curry powder
1 garlic clove, crushed
2 sticks lemongrass, thinly sliced
500 g (1 lb) beef fillet, cut into thin strips
2 tablespoons vegetable oil

1 carrot + ½ cucumber, julienned
100 g (3½ oz) bean sprouts
handful of fresh mint leaves
handful of fresh coriander
100 g (3½ oz) roasted peanuts, crushed

1	Put the fish sauce, 2 tablespoons of water and sugar into a small pan and cook over a low heat until the sugar dissolves. Cool.	2	Cook the noodles in boiling water for 3–5 minutes, or until soft. Drain well, then set aside in cold water.
3	Put the soy sauce, oyster sauce, curry powder, garlic and lemongrass into a bowl, add the beef and mix. Cover and marinate for 30 minutes.	4	Heat the oil in a wok over a high heat and cook the meat in batches until it is browned. ➢

5	Divide the well-drained noodles among 4 serving plates. Top with the carrot, cucumber, bean sprouts, mint and coriander.

TIP

For extra flavour, allow the meat to marinate overnight in the refrigerator.

VARIATION

Cook the meat on the barbecue or chargrill it to add a more traditional flavour.

6	Divide the meat among the plates. Sprinkle with crushed peanuts and drizzle with the cooled fish sauce and sugar mixture.	**VARIATION** ❊ You can use lamb instead of the beef, if you prefer.

TIP
❊

This dish is delicious served either hot or cold.

PORK TONKATSU

⇥ SERVES 4 • PREPARATION: 20 MINUTES • COOKING: 10 MINUTES ⇤

4 pork loin steaks
125 g (4 oz) plain flour
2 eggs, lightly beaten
50 g (2 oz) panko breadcrumbs

groundnut oil, for shallow-frying
150 g (2 oz) shredded cabbage
1 lemon, cut into wedges

TONKATSU SAUCE:
40 ml (1½ fl oz) tomato ketchup
50 ml (2 fl oz) Worcestershire sauce

1	Put one of the pork loin steaks between 2 sheets of cling film.	2	Pound using a mallet until 5 mm (¼ in) thick. Repeat with the other steaks.	3	Dust both sides of each steak lightly with flour, shaking off any excess.
4	Dip the steaks into the beaten egg and press to coat in the breadcrumbs.	5	Heat the oil in a frying pan, add the pork and cook for 3 minutes on each side, or until crisp. Drain.	6	Whisk the ketchup and Worcestershire sauce and serve with sliced pork, cabbage and lemon wedges.

MASAMAN BEEF

❧ SERVES 4 • PREPARATION: 20 MINUTES • COOKING: 25 MINUTES ❦

2 potatoes
1 tablespoon vegetable oil
3 tablespoons Masaman curry paste
500 g (1 lb) rump steak, cubed

1 onion, chopped
500 ml (17 fl oz) coconut milk
2 tablespoons grated palm sugar
2 tablespoons fish sauce

3 tablespoons tamarind concentrate (purée)
3 tablespoons roasted peanuts, chopped
steamed jasmine rice, to serve

1	Cut the potatoes into large pieces then steam or parboil.	2	Heat the oil in a wok, add the curry paste and cook gently for 3 minutes, or until fragrant.	3	Increase the heat to medium. Add the potatoes, steak and onion and cook until the steak browns.
4	Stir in the milk, sugar and fish sauce. Boil, then simmer for 10 minutes.	5	Add the tamarind and cook for another 5 minutes.	6	Top with the chopped roasted peanuts and serve with steamed jasmine rice.

BEEF RENDANG

✦ SERVES 6 • PREPARATION: 20 MINUTES + 30 MINUTES MARINATING • COOKING: 1¾ HOURS ✦

50 g (2 oz) large dried red chillies
1 teaspoon coriander seeds
1 tablespoon chopped fresh ginger
2 teaspoons ground cumin
½ teaspoon ground cloves

¼ teaspoon turmeric
3 garlic cloves, peeled
10 red Asian shallots, roughly chopped
1 kg (2 lb) beef topside, cubed
25 g (1 oz) desiccated coconut

500 ml (17 fl oz) coconut milk
2 stalks lemongrass
1 tablespoon chopped galangal
2 teaspoons grated palm sugar
freshly cooked rice, to serve

1	Soak the chillies in boiling water for 15 minutes, or until soft. Drain well and roughly chop.	2	Put the chillies, coriander seeds, ginger, cumin, cloves, turmeric, garlic and shallots into a food-processor.	3	Process to a smooth paste (you may need to add a little water to bring the paste together).	
4	Put the meat into a bowl, add the spice paste and mix. Chill for 30 minutes.	5	Put the meat, coconut, coconut milk, lemongrass, galangal and sugar in a wok.	6	Boil, then lower the heat and simmer for 1½ hours.	➤

| 7 | Continue to cook, stirring continuously, until the curry is dry. | **TIP**
❋
The flavour of this dish improves on standing so it is best made the day before |
| | | **VARIATION**
❋
This is a great recipe to cook in a pressure cooker; allow 20 minutes to cook. |

8	Serve with freshly cooked rice.	VARIATION ※
		This is a mild rendang so if you would like it spicier add some extra dried red chillies to the paste.

TIP ※	SERVING SUGGESTION ※
Rendang is a dry dish so cook the meat until there is hardly any liquid left.	Rendang makes a tasty filling for pies; serve mini pies at parties.

JAPANESE BEEF CURRY

➤ **SERVES 4 • PREPARATION: 15 MINUTES • COOKING: 20 MINUTES** ❖

1 tablespoon vegetable oil
500 g (1 lb) rump steak, cubed
1 onion, chopped
2 potatoes, cut into bite-size pieces

1 carrot, cut into thick slices
1 packet Japanese pork curry mix,
crumbled
freshly cooked rice, to serve

1	Heat the oil in a pan, add the steak and cook until browned. Add the onion and cook over a medium heat for 5 minutes until golden.	2	Add the potatoes, carrot and 500 ml (17 fl oz) water, cover and simmer for 10 minutes, or until the vegetables are soft.
3	Add the crumbled curry mix and cook, stirring, for 5 minutes, or until the sauce is smooth and thickened.	4	Serve with freshly cooked rice.

POULTRY

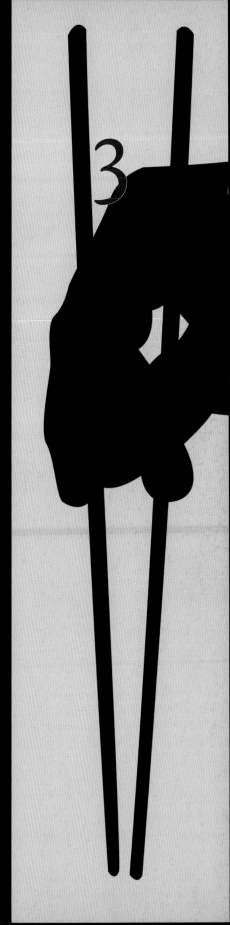

NOODLE DISHES

COCONUT MILK DISHES

STIR-FRIES

CLASSICS

SPICY FRIED CHICKEN

❖ **SERVES 4** • PREPARATION: 15 MINUTES • COOKING: 15 MINUTES ❖

625 g (1¼ lb) cooked udon noodles
1 tablespoon vegetable oil
300 g (10 oz) chicken thigh fillets, sliced
3 spring onions, sliced

1 red pepper, sliced
200 g (7 oz) shiitake mushrooms, sliced
1 bunch pak choi, roughly chopped
100 g (3½ oz) bean sprouts

2 tablespoons sake
3 tablespoons light soy sauce
3 tablespoons sweet chilli sauce
½ teaspoon chilli flakes

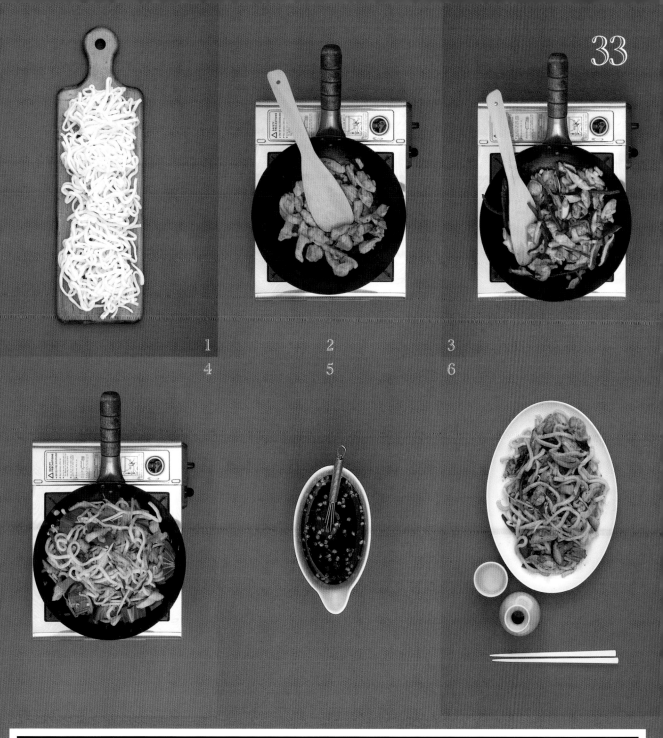

1	Gently separate the noodles.	2	Heat the oil in a wok, add the chicken and cook until it has browned.	3	Add the onions, pepper and mushrooms and cook for 3 minutes.
4	Add the noodles, pak choi and bean sprouts and toss to combine.	5	Whisk the sake, sauces and chilli flakes together. Add to the wok and toss to coat until heated through.	6	Serve immediately.

CHILLI CHICKEN RAMEN

≫ **SERVES 4** • PREPARATION: 5 MINUTES • COOKING: 10 MINUTES ≪

2 chicken breast fillets
1 teaspoon vegetable oil
1 tablespoon chilli sauce

200 g (7 oz) dried ramen or
2-minute noodles
1 bunch pak choi, roughly chopped

1 litre (1¼ pints) hot chicken stock
3 spring onions, sliced

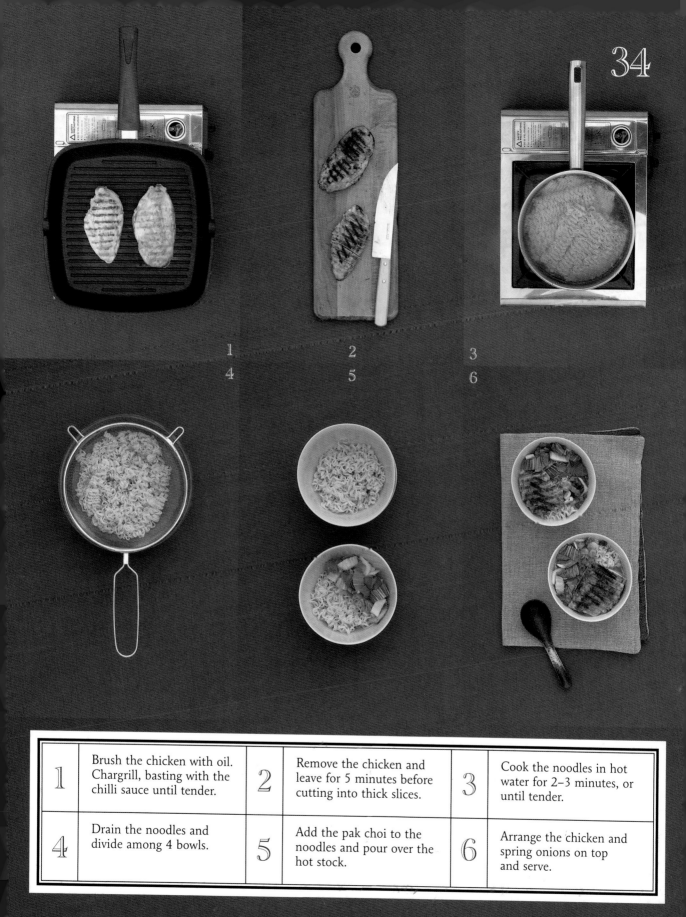

1	Brush the chicken with oil. Chargrill, basting with the chilli sauce until tender.	2	Remove the chicken and leave for 5 minutes before cutting into thick slices.	3	Cook the noodles in hot water for 2–3 minutes, or until tender.
4	Drain the noodles and divide among 4 bowls.	5	Add the pak choi to the noodles and pour over the hot stock.	6	Arrange the chicken and spring onions on top and serve.

CHICKEN PAD THAI

✣ **SERVES 4** • PREPARATION: 30 MINUTES + 15 MINUTES STANDING • COOKING: 15 MINUTES ✣

300 g (10 oz) dried rice stick noodles
2 tablespoons vegetable oil
300 g (10 oz) chicken breast fillets, sliced
100 g (3½ oz) firm tofu, sliced
3 garlic cloves, chopped

2 tablespoons dried prawns (optional)
125 ml (4 fl oz) fish sauce
2 tablespoons caster sugar
75 ml (3 fl oz) tamarind juice
3 eggs, lightly beaten

3 tablespoons chopped roasted peanuts
2 tablespoons garlic chives, cut into
2.5-cm (1-in) pieces
100 g (3½ oz) bean sprouts
1 lime, cut into wedges

1	Put the noodles into a bowl and cover with cold water. Leave for 15 minutes, or until just soft. Drain well.	2	Heat the oil in a wok, add the chicken and tofu and stir-fry over a high heat for 5 minutes, or until the chicken is browned.
3	Add the garlic and dried prawns, if using, and cook for 2 minutes.	4	Add the noodles. Mix the fish sauce, sugar, tamarind juice and 125 ml (4 fl oz) water, and stir-fry for 5 minutes.

| 5 | Push the noodles up one side of the wok, add the eggs and cook, stirring, until the eggs are scrambled. Add the peanuts and chives and combine with the noodles and eggs. | **TIP**
✻

Make sure you soak the noodles in cold water. If you use hot water they will become too soft.

VEGETARIAN ALTERNATIVE
✻

To make vegetarian pad Thai increase the tofu and omit the chicken and prawns. Replace the fish sauce with light soy sauce. |

6	Stir-fry for 2 minutes. Add the bean sprouts and toss to combine. Serve with lime wedges.	**SERVING SUGGESTION** ❈
		Use 250 g (8 oz) chopped peeled fresh prawns if you want to make this dish for a dinner party.
TIP ❈		**TIP** ❈
To reheat any leftover pad Thai add a few tablespoons of water to the wok along with the noodles. This will stop them sticking to the wok.		Be sure to stir-fry the noodles in step 4 until soft.

DUCK & PINEAPPLE CURRY

↦ SERVES 4 • PREPARATION: 15 MINUTES • COOKING: 20 MINUTES ↤

200 ml (7 fl oz) coconut milk, plus the
thick cream at the top of the tin
(do not shake the tin before opening)
2–3 tablespoons red curry paste

1 roast duck, cut into pieces
250 g (8 oz) pineapple, cut into
bite-sized pieces
1 red pepper, chopped

1 tablespoon fish sauce
1 tablespoon grated palm sugar
2 tablespoons fresh Thai basil leaves

1 2
3 4

1	Scoop the thick coconut cream from the top of the tin into a wok and cook until the oil begins to separate from the cream.	2	Add the curry paste and cook for 5 minutes, or until fragrant.
3	Add the coconut milk, duck, pineapple, pepper, fish sauce and sugar and cook for 15 minutes.	4	Scatter with basil leaves before serving.

GREEN CURRY PASTE

✴ MAKES 50 G (2 OZ) • PREPARATION: 5–15 MINUTES • COOKING: 3 MINUTES ✴

½ teaspoon cumin seeds
½ teaspoon coriander seeds
1 star anise
½ teaspoon white peppercorns
1 teaspoon salt

3 garlic cloves
4 lemongrass stalks, peeled
1–2 knobs fresh galangal
2–3 fresh coriander roots
8 Asian shallots, chopped

1 small green chilli
6 large green chillies
handful of fresh coriander leaves
a little vegetable oil, to cover

1	Put the cumin seeds, coriander seeds, star anise and peppercorns in a frying pan and cook for 3 minutes, or until fragrant.	2	Transfer to a food-processor, add the salt, garlic, lemongrass, galangal, coriander roots, shallots, chillies and coriander leaves.
3	Process the mixture to form a smooth paste, scraping down the sides a couple of times.	4	Transfer the paste to a bowl, cover with a little vegetable oil and cover with cling film until ready to use.

CHICKEN GREEN CURRY

❧ SERVES 4 • PREPARATION: 15 MINUTES • COOKING: 20 MINUTES ❧

4 kaffir lime leaves
1 tablespoon palm sugar (optional)
1 tablespoon vegetable oil
2–3 tablespoons green curry paste

500 ml (17 fl oz) coconut milk
500 g (1 lb) chicken thigh fillets
6 small round pea aubergines, quartered

1 tablespoon fish sauce
2 tablespoons fresh Thai basil leaves
freshly cooked rice, to serve

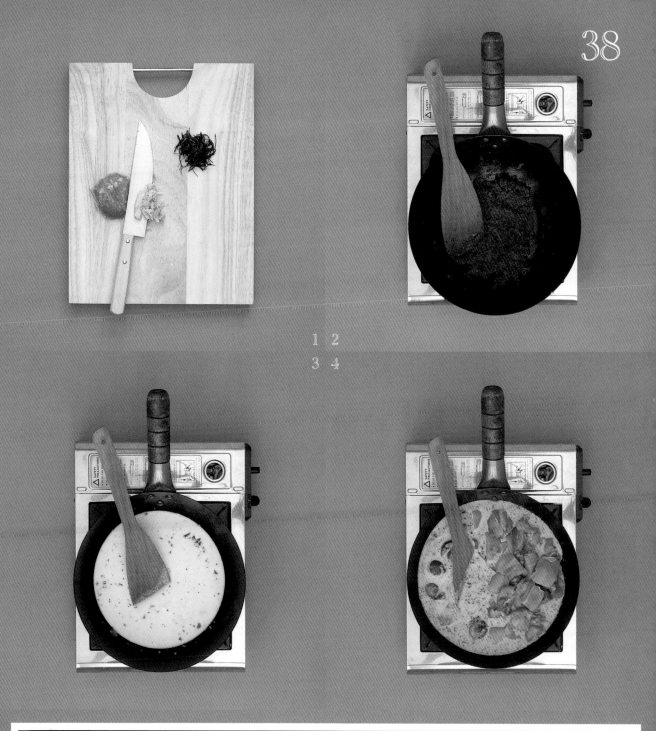

1 2
3 4

1	Finely shred the lime leaves and finely shave or grate the palm sugar, if using.	2	Heat the oil in a pan, add the curry paste and cook until the oil separates from the curry paste.	
3	Add the coconut milk and cook for 5 minutes.	4	Add the chicken, aubergines and lime leaves and simmer for 10 minutes, or until the chicken is tender.	➤

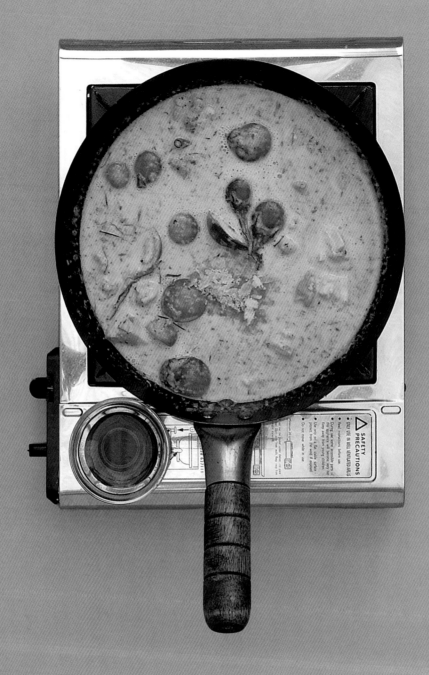

5	Season with fish sauce and the palm sugar.

VARIATION

Any fresh vegetables can be used in this curry, such as snake beans, baby corn, cauliflower or broccoli.

TIP

Curry freezes well. Put it in an airtight container and label with the date. It will keep for 6 weeks.

6 Top the curry with the basil leaves and serve with freshly cooked rice.

TIP

The flavour of curry improves on standing so if you can, make it the day before or in the morning.

TIP

Green curry paste is hotter than red and commercial curry pastes can be quite fiery. I recommend tasting a little bit to gauge its heat – you can always add more at the end if you want it hotter.

VIETNAMESE CHICKEN CURRY

❖ SERVES 4 • PREPARATION: 15 MINUTES + 3 HOURS MARINATING • COOKING: 50 MINUTES ❖

1 knob of galangal
3 lemongrass stalks
3 garlic cloves
1 onion

2 tablespoons curry powder
1.5 kg (3 lb) chicken pieces
2 tablespoons vegetable oil
500 ml (17 fl oz) coconut milk

1 tablespoon caster sugar
500 g (1 lb) potatoes, cut into large pieces
freshly cooked rice, to serve

1	Roughly chop the galangal, lemongrass, garlic and onion.	2	Put the galangal, lemongrass, garlic, onion and curry powder into a food-processor and process to form a smooth paste.	
3	Spread the paste over the chicken, cover and leave to marinate in the fridge for 3 hours.	4	Heat the oil in a large frying pan, add the chicken and cook until browned.	➤

5	Add the coconut milk, sugar, 250 ml (8 fl oz) of water and potatoes. Cover and simmer for 40 minutes, or until the chicken is tender.

VARIATION
❋

You can use all drumsticks for this recipe if you have trouble finding chicken pieces

TIP
❋

You can buy a whole 1.5 kg (3 lb) chicken and cut it into pieces, if you prefer.

6	Serve with freshly cooked rice.	**SERVING SUGGESTION** ❋
		If you are not going to serve this dish immediately, do not add the potatoes. Add them when you reheat the curry to stop them overcooking and breaking up.
	TIP ❋	
	Use a Vietnamese-style curry powder instead of an Indian one, if you can find one.	

STIR-FRIED CHICKEN

❖ SERVES 4 • PREPARATION: 15 MINUTES • COOKING: 10 MINUTES ❖

1 tablespoon vegetable oil
500 g (1 lb) chicken breast fillets, thinly sliced
2 garlic cloves, chopped

1 large red chilli, deseeded and thinly sliced
1 red pepper, thinly sliced
3 spring onions, sliced
1 tablespoon palm sugar

2 tablespoons chilli jam
1 tablespoon fish sauce
handful of fresh Thai basil leaves
freshly cooked rice, to serve

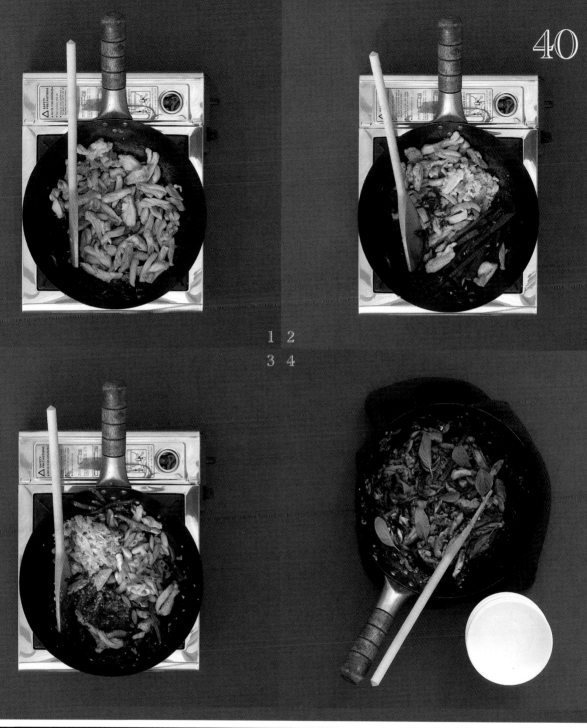

1 2
3 4

1	Heat the oil in a wok, add the chicken and stir-fry until browned.	2	Add the garlic, chilli and pepper and stir-fry until the pepper is soft.
3	Stir in the spring onions, palm sugar, chilli jam and fish sauce. Stir-fry until the sauce is thick and glossy.	4	Remove from the heat, add the basil leaves and serve immediately with freshly cooked rice.

CHICKEN WITH LEMONGRASS

❧ SERVES 4 • PREPARATION: 15 MINUTES • COOKING: 25 MINUTES ❧

5 lemongrass stalks, chopped
2 large red chillies, deseeded and chopped
2 tablespoons vegetable oil

750 g (1½ lb) chicken thigh fillets, cut into bite-sized pieces
1 tablespoon grated palm sugar

3 tablespoons fish sauce
freshly cooked rice, to serve

1	Pound the lemongrass and chilli with a mortar and pestle or put in a food-processor and whiz to a rough paste.	2	Heat the oil in a wok, add the paste and cook over a medium heat for 3 minutes, or until fragrant.
3	Add the chicken and stir-fry for 5 minutes, or until browned. Add the sugar and fish sauce and stir until the sugar begins to caramelize.	4	Serve with freshly cooked rice.

CHICKEN WITH CASHEWS

➤ SERVES 4 · PREPARATION: 15 MINUTES + 30 MINUTES MARINATING · COOKING: 15 MINUTES ⭠

2 tablespoons cornflour
500 g (1 lb) chicken breast fillets,
thinly sliced
2 tablespoons Shaoxing rice wine

2 tablespoons oyster sauce
1 tablespoon vegetable oil
1 onion, cut in half and thinly sliced
2 garlic cloves, chopped

1 carrot, thinly sliced
200 g (7 oz) mangetout
200 g (7 oz) cashews, toasted

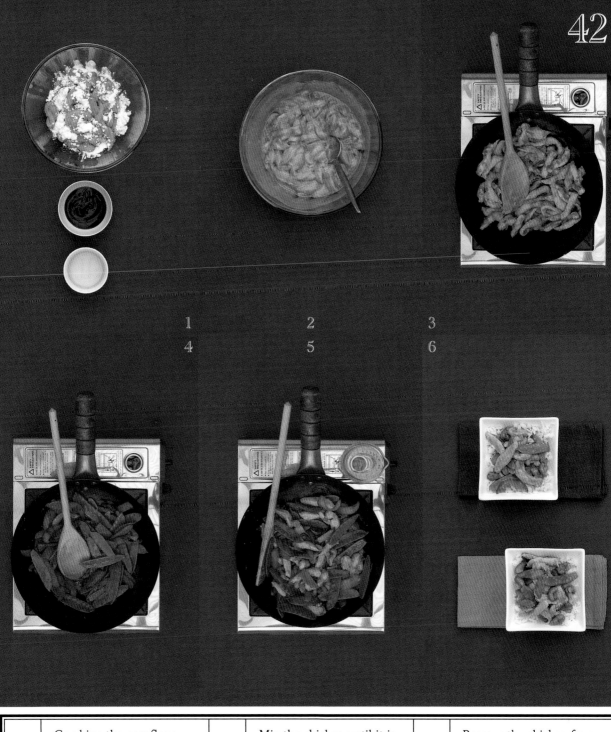

1	Combine the cornflour, chicken, rice wine and oyster sauce.	2	Mix the chicken until it is coated in the marinade and marinate for 30 minutes.	3	Remove the chicken from the marinade. Heat the oil and brown the chicken.
4	Remove the chicken, add the onion and garlic and fry for 3 minutes. Add the vegetables and fry briefly.	5	Return the chicken to the wok with 125 ml (4 fl oz) water and cook, stirring, until thick.	6	Add the cashews and serve.

TERIYAKI CHICKEN

❧ SERVES 1 • PREPARATION: 5 MINUTES • COOKING: 25 MINUTES ❧

8 chicken drumsticks
2 tablespoons vegetable oil
100 ml (3½ fl oz) sake
100 ml (3½ fl oz) mirin

100 ml (3½ fl oz) dark soy sauce
2 teaspoons caster sugar
freshly cooked rice and vegetables, to serve

NOTE: You can cook any cut of chicken, meat or tofu in this way.

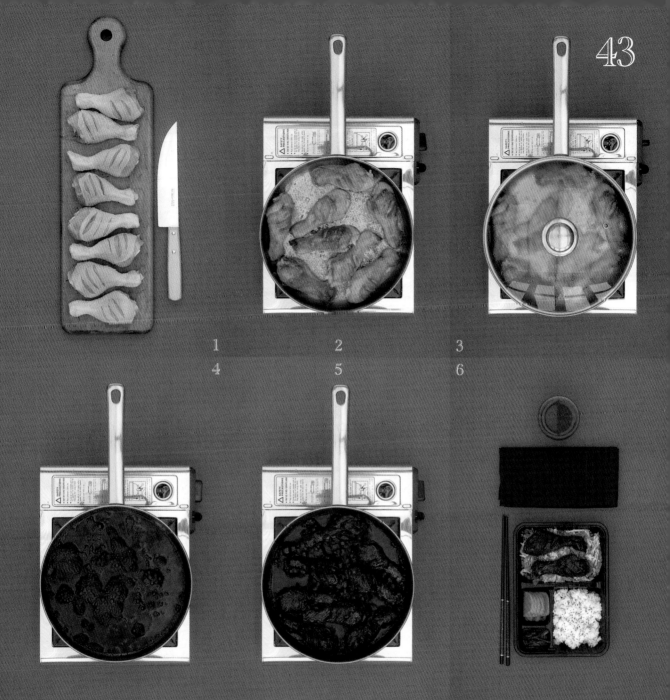

1	Score the chicken legs – this will help them to cook evenly.	2	Heat the oil in a pan, add the chicken and cook for 10 minutes until browned.	3	Cover and cook for another 10 minutes. Remove the chicken from the pan.
4	Add the sake, mirin, soy sauce and sugar and boil until the sauce is glossy.	5	Return the chicken to the pan and cook until it is coated in the sauce.	6	Serve the chicken with rice and vegetables and any extra sauce.

VIETNAMESE CHICKEN SALAD

❖ SERVES 4 • PREPARATION: 15 MINUTES + 30 MINUTES MARINATING • COOKING: 20 MINUTES ❖

125 ml (4 fl oz) rice vinegar
2 tablespoons caster sugar
1 red onion, thinly sliced

sea salt and black pepper
2 chicken breast fillets
250 g (8 oz) Chinese cabbage, shredded

1 carrot, julienned
20 g (¾ oz) fresh Vietnamese mint
50 g (2 oz) fried chopped Asian shallots

1	Mix the vinegar and sugar together, add the onion, season with salt and pepper and leave for 30 minutes.	2	Put the chicken in a frying pan, add enough water to just cover and cook gently for 15–20 minutes.	3	Remove and leave to cool before shredding.
4	Put the cabbage, carrot, mint and chicken in a small bowl.	5	Add the onion and vinegar mixture and toss well to combine.	6	Serve topped with fried Asian shallots.

YAKITORI CHICKEN

✦ SERVES 4 • PREPARATION: 20 MINUTES ✦ 15 MINUTES SOAKING • COOKING: 20 MINUTES ✦

100 ml (3½ fl oz) sake
125 ml (4 fl oz) light soy sauce
3 tablespoons mirin

2 tablespoons caster sugar
1 kg (2 lb) chicken thigh fillets
8 spring onions

1	Soak several bamboo skewers in cold water for 15 minutes.	2	Bring the sake, soy, mirin and sugar to the boil and cook for 5 minutes. Cool.	3	Cut the chicken into thick strips and the spring onions into 5-cm (2-in) pieces.
4	Thread the chicken and the spring onions onto the presoaked skewers.	5	Chargrill the chicken until tender, dipping the skewers in the sauce a couple of times during cooking.	6	Serve the chicken with the remaining sauce.

PEKING DUCK

❖ SERVES 1 6 • PREPARATION: 15 MINUTES • COOKING: 5 MINUTES ❖

6 spring onions
1 roast, glazed duck (see tip)
12 spring onion pancakes

125 ml (4 fl oz) hoisin sauce
½ cucumber, cut into batons

1	Cut the top of the spring onions into thin strips without cutting all the way through and stand in a glass of iced water.	2	Using a sharp knife, slice the skin from the duck.
3	Put the pancakes in a steamer, cover and steam over a wok of simmering water.	4	Lay the pancakes in front of each dinner guest and let them spoon a little hoisin sauce into the centre of the pancakes. ➤

5	Top with some duck skin, a piece of spring onion and cucumber.	**TIP** ※ The pancakes can be found in the freezer section of Asian food stores.
	TIP ※ Purchase your duck from Chinatown or an Asian food store.	**SERVING SUGGESTION** ※ To get the duck skin crisp, reheat it in an oven at 220°C (425°F), Gas Mark 7 for 20 minutes. When it is cool enough to handle, carefully remove the skin.

6	Roll up and eat immediately.	**TIP** ❋ The duck carcass can be boiled in hot water to make a delicious stock.
	TIP ❋ Use the chopped leftover duck meat to make Sung Choi Bau (see recipe 20).	**TIP** ❋ Use your homemade stock for soup or risotto.

MARINATED CHICKEN WINGS

✦ SERVES 6 • PREPARATION: 20 MINUTES + 4–8 HOURS MARINATING • COOKING: 40 MINUTES ✦

1 kg (2 lb) chicken wings
1 teaspoon sesame oil
3 tablespoons soy sauce

2 tablespoons sweet chilli sauce
2 tablespoons kecap manis
1 tablespoon lemon juice

| 1 2 |
| 3 4 |

1	Use a cleaver to remove the tips from the chicken wings.	2	Cut the wings through the centre joint.	
3	Put the sesame oil, soy sauce, sweet chilli sauce, kecap manis and lemon juice in a bowl and mix to combine.	4	Add the chicken and toss to coat in the marinade. Cover and set aside in the refrigerator for 4 hours, or overnight.	➤

| 5 | Preheat the oven to 220°C (425°F), Gas Mark 7. Arrange the chicken in a baking dish and cook for 10 minutes, turning halfway during the cooking process. | **VARIATION** ❋

 You can use chicken drumsticks instead of wings, if you prefer, and cook in the oven for 50 minutes. |

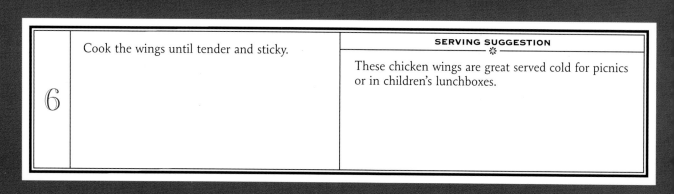

| 6 | Cook the wings until tender and sticky. | **SERVING SUGGESTION**
❋
These chicken wings are great served cold for picnics or in children's lunchboxes. |

CRISPY SPICED DUCK

SERVES 4 • PREPARATION: 15 MINUTES • COOKING: 30 MINUTES

4 duck breasts, skin on
2 tablespoons plain flour
¼ teaspoon five-spice powder
½ teaspoon chilli powder

1 teaspoon sea salt
groundnut oil, for deep-frying
3 spring onions, sliced
tenderstem broccoli, to serve

PLUM SAUCE
250 ml (8 fl oz) plum sauce
1–2 tablespoons rice vinegar

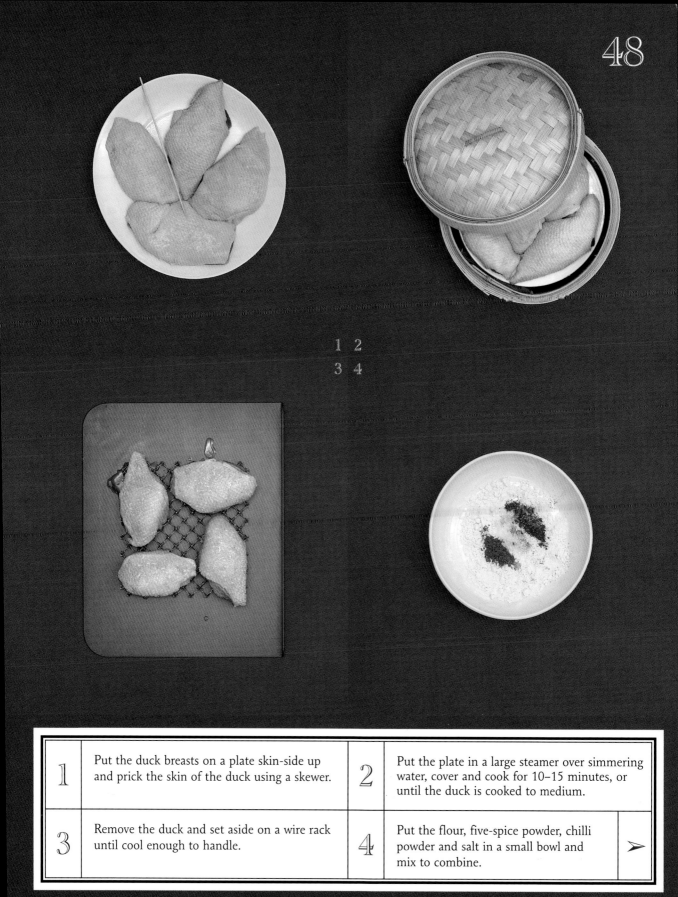

1	2
3	4

1	Put the duck breasts on a plate skin-side up and prick the skin of the duck using a skewer.	2	Put the plate in a large steamer over simmering water, cover and cook for 10–15 minutes, or until the duck is cooked to medium.	
3	Remove the duck and set aside on a wire rack until cool enough to handle.	4	Put the flour, five-spice powder, chilli powder and salt in a small bowl and mix to combine.	➤

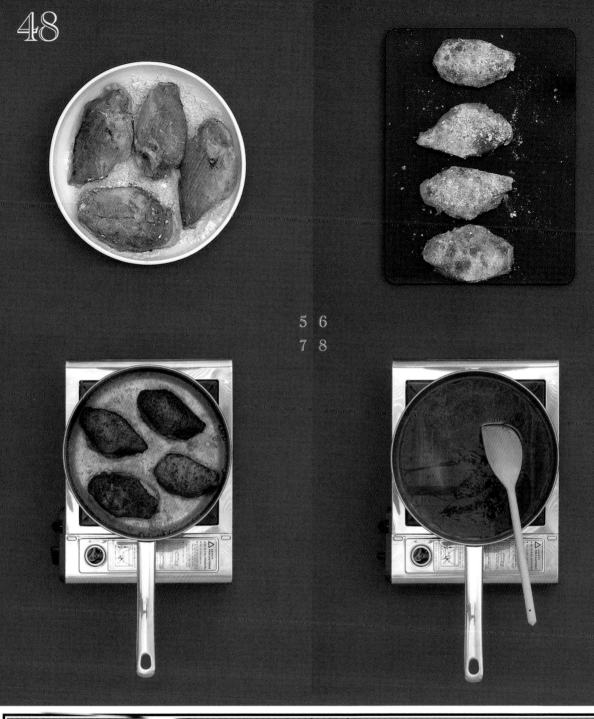

5 6
7 8

5	Coat both sides of the duck in the spiced flour mixture.	6	Shake off any excess flour.
7	Heat the oil and deep-fry the duck breasts for 3 minutes, or until the skin is crisp and golden. Cut into thin slices.	8	Heat the plum sauce and rice vinegar together until boiling.

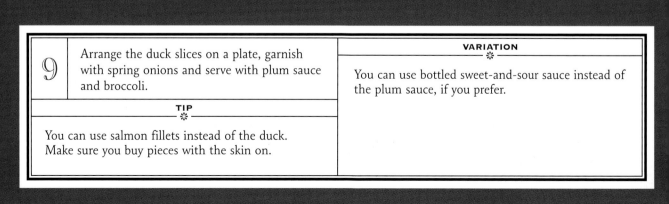

9   Arrange the duck slices on a plate, garnish with spring onions and serve with plum sauce and broccoli.

TIP
❈

You can use salmon fillets instead of the duck. Make sure you buy pieces with the skin on.

VARIATION
❈

You can use bottled sweet-and-sour sauce instead of the plum sauce, if you prefer.

NASI GORENG

⮞ SERVES 4 • PREPARATION: 20 MINUTES • COOKING: 10 MINUTES ⮜

1 tablespoon groundnut oil
1 teaspoon sambal oelek
2 garlic cloves, crushed
250 g (8 oz) skinless chicken thigh fillets,
finely chopped

250 g (8 oz) peeled raw prawns,
finely chopped
3 spring onions, sliced
750 g (1½ lb) cold cooked rice
1 tablespoon kecap manis

1 tablespoon gluten-free soy sauce
(tamari)
4 eggs
2 tomatoes, sliced
½ cucumber, sliced

1 2
3 4

1	Heat the oil in a wok, add the sambal oelek, garlic, chicken and prawns and stir-fry until the chicken is golden.	2	Add the spring onions and rice and stir-fry for 5 minutes, or until the rice is heated through.
3	Combine the sauces, stir in and cook until hot. Remove from the wok and cover. Fry the eggs one at a time in the wok.	4	Serve a mound of rice mixture topped with the egg and accompanied by the sliced tomatoes and cucumber.

SEAFOOD

QUICK & EASY DISHES

SIMPLE MAIN DISHES

RICE & NOODLE DISHES

SUSHI

SWEET CHILLI SQUID SALAD

❋ SERVES 4 • PREPARATION TIME: 20 MINUTES • COOKING: 10 MINUTES ❋

300 g (1 lb) cleaned baby squid, tentacles
removed
1 tablespoon vegetable oil
3 tablespoons sweet chilli sauce
1 tablespoon fish sauce

1 tablespoon lime juice
150 g (5 oz) mixed salad leaves
50 g (2 oz) bean sprouts
1 cucumber, thinly sliced

1	Cut the squid pouches in half and lay them skin-side down on a board.	2	Score the squid by cutting diagonally in one direction, taking care not to cut all the way through.
3	Turn the board and cut in the other direction. Cut into small pieces.	4	Heat the oil in a wok until it starts to smoke. Add the squid and cook until it starts to curl up. ➢

5	Combine the sweet chilli sauce, fish sauce and lime juice and add to the wok. Cook until sticky.	**VARIATION** ❈
		Use peeled tiger prawns instead of the squid.

VARIATION ❈	**TIP** ❈
Use ordinary squid instead of the baby squid	The squid in the sauce can be used for a stir-fry – add some mangetout, broccoli and asparagus.

6	Arrange the salad leaves on a platter, top with the bean sprouts and cucumber, and finish with the squid.	**TIP** ❈ To save time, slice the squid pouches into rings.
SERVING SUGGESTION ❈ This can be cooked on the barbecue on a flat griddle. You might want to double the sauce ingredients.		**SERVING SUGGESTION** ❈ This is a great dish to serve at a party in small Chinese take-away boxes.

ASIAN OYSTERS

❖ MAKES 24 • PREPARATION. 15 MINUTES • COOKING: 2 MINUTES ❖

2 lup cheong (Chinese sausages)
24 shucked oysters
1 tablespoon Worcestershire sauce
1 tablespoon grated palm sugar

1 tablespoon fish sauce
1 tablespoon lime juice
1 large red chilli, deseeded and
finely chopped

1 2
3 4

1	Finely chop the lup cheong sausage.	2	Arrange 12 of the oysters on a board. Put the remaining oysters onto a baking tray. Top with the Worcestershire sauce and lup cheong.	
3	Whisk together the sugar, fish sauce, lime juice and chilli.	4	Divide the dressing among the uncooked oysters on the board.	➤

5	Grill the oysters on the baking tray under a preheated grill on high for 2 minutes, or until the sausage is crisp.

SERVING SUGGESTION
❋

This topping also works well on halved mussels or you can serve a combination of the two.

6 Serve the cooked and uncooked oysters immediately.	**SERVING SUGGESTION** ❋ Serve the fresh oysters drizzled with a little chilli oil, light soy sauce, chopped spring onions and some shredded ginger.
VARIATION ❋ Try steaming the raw oysters then serve immediately with the dressing.	

MUSSELS WITH LEMONGRASS

❧ **SERVES 4 • PREPARATION: 15 MINUTES • COOKING: 10 MINUTES** ❧

1 kg (2 lb) live mussels
2 tablespoons vegetable oil
3 lemongrass stalks, thinly sliced
2 tablespoons finely shredded fresh ginger

125 ml (4 fl oz) fish stock
1 tablespoon fish sauce
1 large red chilli, deseeded and thinly sliced
handful fresh coriander sprigs

3 spring onions, sliced
juice from 1–2 limes

1

2

3

4

5

6

1	Scrub and debeard the mussels, discarding any that are open.	2	Heat the oil in a wok, add the lemongrass and ginger and cook for 2 minutes.	3	Add the mussels and toss to coat them in the lemongrass mixture.
4	Mix the stock and fish sauce together, then pour into the wok.	5	Cover and cook until the mussels open. Discard any that do not open.	6	Transfer the mussels to a bowl and top with the remaining ingredients.

SALT & PEPPER SQUID

⇶ **SERVES 4–6** • PREPARATION: 30 MINUTES • COOKING TIME 10 MINUTES ⇶

1 kg (2 lb) baby squid
4 tablespoons sea salt
3 tablespoons white peppercorns
2 teaspoons caster sugar

125 g (4 oz) cornflour
125 g (4 oz) plain flour
4 egg whites, lightly beaten
groundnut oil, for deep-frying

TO SERVE:
lemon wedges
soy sauce

1	Clean the squid. Cut the pouches into rings and the tentacles in half.	2	Put the salt, peppercorns and sugar into a mortar and pestle and grind to a fine powder.	3	Transfer to a bowl, add the cornflour and flour and mix to combine.
4	Coat the squid in the egg whites, then toss in the seasoned flour until coated.	5	Heat the oil in a wok and fry the squid for 2 minutes, or until crisp. Drain.	6	Serve the squid with lemon wedges and soy sauce.

SEAFOOD RED CURRY

⇒ **SERVES 4** • PREPARATION: 10 MINUTES • COOKING: 25 MINUTES ⇐

125 g (4 oz) can bamboo shoots, rinsed
and drained
500 g (1 lb) raw tiger prawns
250 g (8 oz) boneless white fish fillets
200 g (7 oz) fresh scallops

2 tablespoons vegetable oil
2–3 tablespoons Thai red curry paste
2 teaspoons shrimp paste (optional)
500 ml (17 fl oz) coconut milk
1 tablespoon fish sauce

1 tablespoon grated palm sugar
4 kaffir lime leaves, finely shredded
200 g (7 oz) French beans, trimmed
steamed jasmine rice, to serve

1 2
3 4

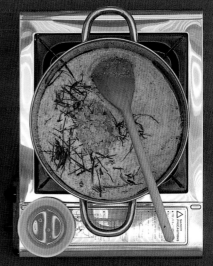

1	Cut the bamboo shoots into thin strips.	2	Peel and devein the prawns, cut the fish into bite-sized pieces and pat the scallops dry with kitchen paper.	
3	Heat the oil in a pan, add the curry paste and shrimp paste, if using, and cook over a medium heat until the oil separates from the curry paste.	4	Add the coconut milk, fish sauce, sugar and lime leaves, bring to the boil, then lower the heat and cook for 10 minutes.	➤

| 5 | Add the bamboo shoots and beans and cook for 5 minutes. Add the seafood and cook for another 5 minutes, or until the fish is tender. | **VARIATION**
※
Use a combination of seafood for this recipe or just use one type, if you prefer.

TIP
※
If you are cooking this curry ahead of time, do not add the seafood until you are ready to serve; this way the fish will not break up. |

| 6 | Serve with steamed jasmine rice. | **VARIATION**
❈

You can use sliced bamboo shoots instead of whole ones, if you prefer.

TIP
❈

Commercial curry pastes do vary in temperature, so it is better to start with a little less than the recipe specifies if you are using a paste for the first time. |

STEAMED FISH WITH GINGER

❖ SERVES 4 • PREPARATION: 10 MINUTES • COOKING: 20 MINUTES ❖

10-cm (4-in) piece fresh ginger
750 g (1½ lb) boneless white fish fillets,
such as red snapper, sea bass or cod
3 tablespoons Shaoxing rice wine

3 tablespoons light soy sauce
1 tablespoon caster sugar
2 tablespoons groundnut oil
1 teaspoon sesame oil

2 spring onions, finely sliced
a few fresh coriander sprigs
freshly steamed pak choi, to serve

1	Peel and finely shred the ginger.	2	Put the fish on a large plate and sprinkle with the ginger.
3	Put the rice wine, soy sauce and sugar in a bowl and mix to combine.	4	Pour the rice wine mixture over the fish. Heat the oils in a pan until smoking, then pour over the fish. ➤

5	Put into a steamer over simmering water, then cover and steam for 15–20 minutes, or until the fish flakes easily.	**TIP** ❋ If you are watching your weight, simply steam the fish and serve with the dressing.
VARIATION ❋ Try steaming fresh prawns or scallops and serving them with this dressing.		**SERVING SUGGESTION** ❋ You can cook Asian green vegetables in a steamer on top at the same time to serve with the fish.

6	Top with the spring onions and coriander and serve with pak choi.

VARIATION

❊

Substitute chicken for the fish if you prefer.

TIP

❊

You will need a large bamboo steamer for this recipe. Alternatively, use a smaller layered steamer and cook the fish fillets on individual plates.

SCALLOPS & MANGETOUT

➤ SERVES 4 • PREPARATION: 10 MINUTES • COOKING: 10 MINUTES ➤

1 tablespoon vegetable oil
2 garlic cloves, chopped
1 tablespoon grated fresh ginger
2 spring onions, sliced

300 g (10 oz) fresh scallops
200 g (7 oz) mangetout
2 tablespoons Shaoxing rice wine
1 tablespoon light soy sauce

3 tablespoons chicken stock
freshly cooked rice, to serve

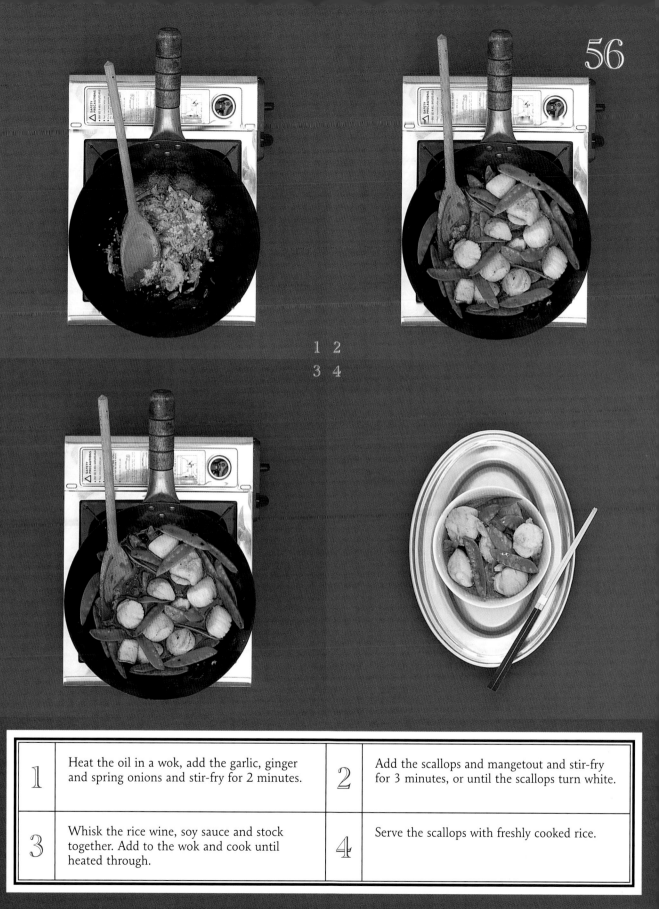

1	Heat the oil in a wok, add the garlic, ginger and spring onions and stir-fry for 2 minutes.	2	Add the scallops and mangetout and stir-fry for 3 minutes, or until the scallops turn white.
3	Whisk the rice wine, soy sauce and stock together. Add to the wok and cook until heated through.	4	Serve the scallops with freshly cooked rice.

CLAY POT SALMON

✦ SERVES 2 • PREPARATION: 10 MINUTES • COOKING: 20 MINUTES ✦

1 tablespoon vegetable oil
2 salmon fillets, about 200 g (7 oz) each
1 tablespoons brown sugar

1 tablespoons fish sauce
2 spring onions, thinly sliced
freshly cooked rice, to serve

NOTE:
If you do not have a clay pot you can use
a frying pan with a lid or a heavy-based
casserole dish

1	Heat the oil in a frying pan until smoking, add the salmon and cook until the skin is crisp. Remove and transfer to a clay pot or casserole.	2	Add the sugar and fish sauce to the pan and cook over a low heat until the sugar has completely dissolved.
3	Pour the caramel sauce into the clay pot, cover and simmer for 15 minutes, or until the salmon is cooked to your liking.	4	Serve sprinkled with spring onions and accompanied by freshly cooked rice.

FISH WITH MISO

➤ **SERVES 4** • PREPARATION: 10 MINUTES + 10 MINUTES SOAKING • COOKING: 20 MINUTES ➤

4 dried Chinese mushrooms
200 g (7 oz) soba noodles
25 g (1 oz) butter
2 tablespoons sake

2 tablespoons mirin
1 tablespoon soy sauce
1 tablespoon caster sugar
3 tablespoons yellow miso

4 pieces boneless firm white fish fillets,
such as snapper or cod
2 spring onions, thinly sliced
freshly cooked rice, to serve

1 2
3 4

1	Preheat the oven to 220°C (425°F), Gas Mark 7. Soak the mushrooms in hot water for 10 minutes. Drain and finely shred the caps.	2	Cook the noodles in boiling water until just tender, then drain well.	
3	Put the butter, sake, mirin, soy sauce and sugar into a pan and bring to the boil. Remove from the heat and stir in the miso.	4	Cut 4 squares of aluminium foil and put a mound of noodles in the centre. Top with the fish, onions and mushrooms.	➤

5	Pour the sauce over the top and fold in the sides to enclose the parcel. Put on a non-stick baking tray and cook in the oven for 15 minutes, or until the fish is tender.	**VARIATION** ❋ Use chicken or tofu instead of the fish. **TIP** ❋ Drain the mushrooms in step 1, then remove and discard the stalks before shredding the caps.

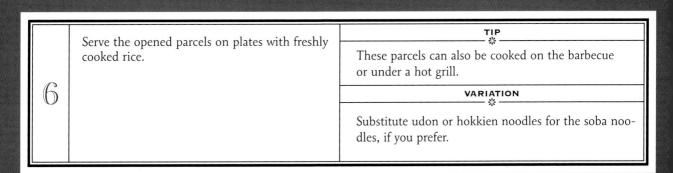

| 6 | Serve the opened parcels on plates with freshly cooked rice. | **TIP**
❋

These parcels can also be cooked on the barbecue or under a hot grill.

VARIATION
❋

Substitute udon or hokkien noodles for the soba noodles, if you prefer. |

SEAFOOD NOODLES

⇾ **SERVES 4 • PREPARATION: 15 MINUTES • COOKING: 15 MINUTES** ⇽

300 g (10 oz) baby squid
300 g (10 oz) raw prawns
12 fresh scallops
1 tablespoon vegetable oil
1 teaspoon sesame oil

5 spring onions, thinly sliced
1 tablespoon finely shredded fresh ginger
1 red pepper, sliced
400 g (13 oz) fresh hokkien noodles
2 tablespoons oyster sauce

2 tablespoons soy sauce
2 tablespoons kecap manis
1 bunch pak choi, finely chopped

1 2
3 4

1	Clean the squid and cut the pouch into rings. Cut the tentacles in half. Peel and devein the prawns. Pat the scallops dry with kitchen paper.	2	Heat the oils in a wok over a high heat. Add the spring onions, ginger and pepper and cook for 3 minutes. Add the seafood and stir-fry over a high heat for 3 minutes, or until it changes colour.
3	Add the noodles, oyster sauce, soy sauce and kecap manis, then stir in the pak choi.	4	Stir-fry until the sauce is thick and glossy and the pak choi has wilted. Serve immediately.

FRIED RICE WITH PRAWNS

❖ SERVES 4 • PREPARATION: 15 MINUTES • COOKING: 15 MINUTES ❖

500 g (1 lb) raw tiger prawns
3 tablespoons vegetable oil
3 eggs, lightly beaten

2 lup cheong (Chinese sausages) or 2 bacon
rashers, chopped
1 tablespoon grated fresh ginger
750 g (1½ lb) cooked and cooled white rice

2 tablespoons Shaoxing rice wine
2 tablespoons soy sauce
3 spring onions, sliced

1	Peel and devein the prawns and roughly chop.	2	Heat half the oil in a wok, add the eggs and swirl to coat the base of the pan. Cook until set.	3	Remove the omelette from the wok, roll up and cut into thin shreds.
4	Heat the remaining oil, add the prawns, lup cheong and ginger and stir-fry briefly.	5	Add the rice, rice wine and soy sauce and stir until heated through.	6	Add the spring onions and toss until combined and hot. Serve.

CHIRASHI SUSHI

✦ SERVES 4 • PREPARATION: 20 MINUTES • COOKING: 20 MINUTES ✦

1 tablespoon vegetable oil
2 eggs, lightly beaten
875 g (1¾ lb) prepared sushi rice
(see recipe 03)

1 sheet nori (seaweed), finely shredded
200 g (7 oz) sashimi-grade salmon,
thinly sliced
200 g (7 oz) sashimi-grade tuna, thinly sliced

½ cucumber, sliced
½ teaspoon wasabi
100 g (3½ oz) pickled ginger

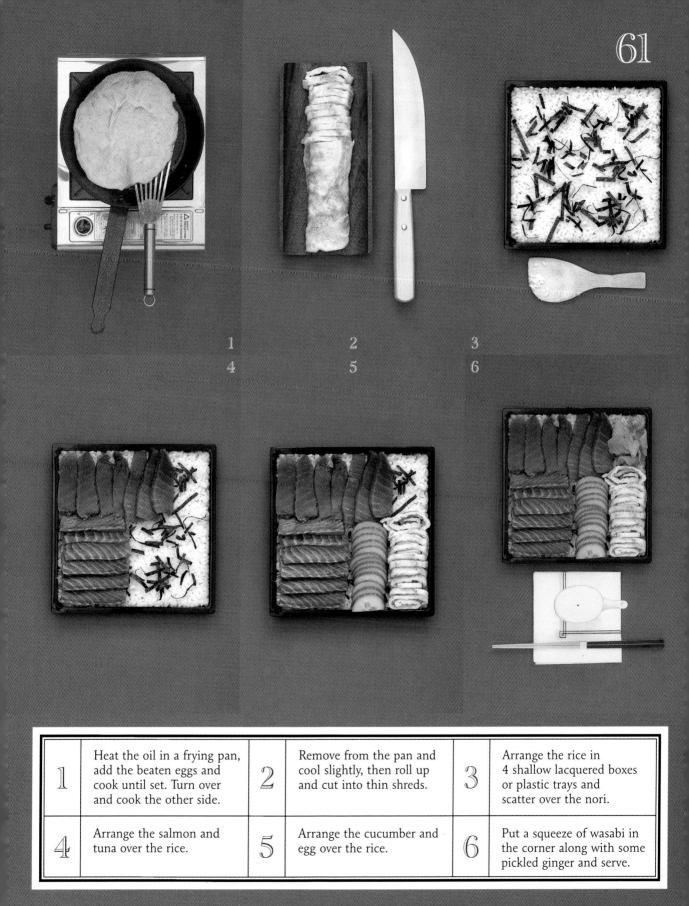

1	Heat the oil in a frying pan, add the beaten eggs and cook until set. Turn over and cook the other side.	2	Remove from the pan and cool slightly, then roll up and cut into thin shreds.	3	Arrange the rice in 4 shallow lacquered boxes or plastic trays and scatter over the nori.
4	Arrange the salmon and tuna over the rice.	5	Arrange the cucumber and egg over the rice.	6	Put a squeeze of wasabi in the corner along with some pickled ginger and serve.

TEMAKI SUSHI

➹ **SERVES 4** • PREPARATION: 15 MINUTES • COOKING: NIL IF YOU HAVE PREPARED THE RICE ➷

300 g (10 oz) skinless salmon fillet
½ cucumber
1 avocado

4 sheets roasted nori (seaweed)
440 g (14 oz) seasoned sushi rice
(see recipe 03)

¼ teaspoon wasabi, plus extra to serve
(optional)
soy sauce, to serve (optional)

1 2
3 4

1	Cut the salmon into thin strips with a sharp knife. Cut the cucumber and avocado into thin strips the same size as the salmon.	2	Cut the nori sheets in half then in half again.
3	Put a tablespoon of cooked rice onto the centre of each piece of nori. Top with a little wasabi, salmon, cucumber and avocado strips.	4	Roll up the nori to form a cone shape and serve with soy sauce and extra wasabi, if you like.

VEGETABLES

DEEP-FRIED

CURRIES

EGGS

SIDE DISHES

AGEDASHI TOFU

✤ SERVES 4 • PREPARATION: 15 MINUTES + 15 MINUTES DRAINING • COOKING: 10 MINUTES ✤

500 g (1 lb) silken firm tofu
plain flour, for dusting
1 teaspoon dashi granules

2 tablespoons light soy sauce
2 tablespoons mirin
groundnut oil, for deep-frying

TO SERVE:
2 tablespoons bonito flakes
2 spring onions, finely shredded
freshly cooked rice

1	Put the tofu on kitchen paper on a board. Cover with paper and a board. Leave for 15 minutes.	2	Cut the tofu into 1-cm (½-in) thick rectangles and pat dry with kitchen paper.	3	Lightly coat both sides of the tofu with the flour, shaking off any excess.
4	Cook the dashi, soy and mirin in 500 ml (17 fl oz) boiling water for 5 minutes.	5	Heat the oil and cook the tofu until crisp and golden. Drain on kitchen paper.	6	Serve the tofu with the broth, bonito flakes, spring onions and rice.

VEGETABLE TEMPURA

SERVES 4 • PREPARATION: 15 MINUTES • COOKING: 15 MINUTES

DIPPING SAUCE:
⅛ teaspoon dashi granules
2 tablespoons mirin
2 tablespoons light soy sauce

TEMPURA BATTER:
2 egg yolks
500 ml (17 fl oz) chilled water
250 g (8 oz) plain flour
200 g (7 oz) sweet potato, julienned

1 onion, thinly sliced
1 red pepper, thinly sliced
100 g (3½ oz) shiitake mushrooms
100 g (3½ oz) green beans, trimmed
vegetable oil, for deep-frying

1 2
3 4

1	For the sauce, put the dashi, 2 tablespoons of water, mirin and soy sauce in a pan and heat until boiling. Cool to room temperature.	2	For the batter, whisk the egg yolks and the chilled water together in a bowl. Sift in the flour and stir until just combined.
3	Put the sweet potato and onion in a bowl. Add half the tempura batter and roughly mix.	4	Dip the remaining vegetables in the batter, allowing any excess to drain off. ➤

5	Divide the sweet potato mixture into 50 g (2 oz) portions. Heat the oil and deep-fry the sweet potato mixture until crisp and golden. Drain on kitchen paper.	**TIP** ❋
		To make a very light batter use chilled soda water instead of the water.
		VARIATION ❋
		Use any vegetables for the tempura, such as baby spinach leaves, mangetout and baby corn.

6	Cook the vegetables in the hot oil until crisp and golden. Serve the tempura on a plate with the dipping sauce on the side.	**TIP** ❋ It is best to deep-fry the tempura in batches and to drain on kitchen paper before serving.
		SERVING SUGGESTION ❋ Double the dipping sauce ingredients and keep chilled to serve as a dressing for chilled soba noodles.

VEGETABLE GREEN CURRY

SERVES 4 • PREPARATION: 15 MINUTES • COOKING: 30 MINUTES

1 tablespoon vegetable oil
2 tablespoons green curry paste
200 g (7 oz) firm tofu, cut into cubes
500 ml (17 fl oz) coconut milk

4 kaffir lime leaves, finely shredded
1 red pepper, sliced
1 courgette, sliced
100 g (3½ oz) baby corn

200 g (7 oz) button mushrooms, halved
1 tablespoon grated palm sugar
1 tablespoon lime juice
freshly cooked rice, to serve

1 2
3 4

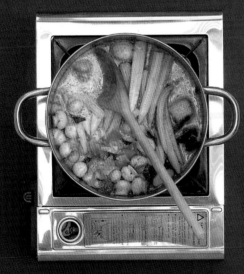

1	Heat the oil in a pan, add the curry paste and cook until the oil comes away from the paste.	2	Add the tofu and cook until browned.
3	Add the coconut milk, lime leaves and vegetables and cook for 20 minutes, or until the vegetables are tender.	4	Season with palm sugar and lime juice and serve with freshly cooked rice.

SATAY PUMPKIN CURRY

⋇ SERVES 4 • PREPARATION: 15 MINUTES • COOKING: 30 MINUTES ⋇

1 tablespoon vegetable oil
2 tablespoons satay paste
2 tablespoons grated fresh ginger
300 g (1 lb) pumpkin, peeled and cut into chunks

200 g (7 oz) firm tofu, drained and cut into cubes
200 g (7 oz) tomatoes
500 ml (17 fl oz) coconut cream
100 g (3½ oz) baby spinach leaves

2 tablespoons chopped fresh coriander
freshly cooked rice, to serve

1 2
3 4

1	Heat the oil in a pan, add the satay paste and ginger and cook over a medium heat for 3 minutes, or until the oil starts to separate from the satay paste.	2	Add the pumpkin and cook until it is coated in the paste and softened slightly.
3	Add the tofu, tomatoes and coconut cream. Bring to the boil, then lower the heat and cook for 20 minutes until the pumpkin is tender.	4	Stir in the spinach and coriander and serve with freshly cooked rice.

CHINESE VEGETABLE OMELETTE

SERVES 2 • PREPARATION: 15 MINUTES • COOKING: 10 MINUTES

6 eggs
3 spring onions, sliced
1 tablespoon light soy sauce

2 tablespoons vegetable oil
100 g (3¼ oz) shiitake mushrooms, sliced
1 tomato, chopped

½ bunch pak choi, roughly chopped
50 g (2 oz) bean sprouts
1 tablespoon kecap manis

| 1 | 2 |
| 3 | 4 |

1	Whisk together the eggs, spring onions and soy sauce.	2	Heat half the oil in a wok, add the mushrooms and stir-fry for 5 minutes, or until browned. Remove from the wok.	
3	Heat the remaining oil in the wok, add the egg mixture and swirl to cover the base of the wok.	4	Cook until nearly set, then add the mushrooms, tomato, pak choi and bean sprouts.	➤

5	Fold the omelette in half to enclose the filling.	**VARIATION** ❋ These omelettes are also delicious filled with fried rice.
TIP ❋ You can make smaller individual omelettes rather than a large one, if you prefer.		**VARIATION** ❋ Use any vegetable for the filling and add some fried tofu or some cooked egg noodles.

6	Fold the omelette in half again and remove from the wok. Drizzle with kecap manis and serve.	**SERVING SUGGESTION** ❋
		These omelettes can be served for breakfast, lunch or as an easy supper.

VARIATION ❋	**TIP** ❋
Use oyster sauce instead of kecap manis, if you prefer.	Make sure the oil is hot before adding the egg mixture in step 3.

GADO GADO

↳ SERVES 4 • PREPARATION: 20 MINUTES • COOKING: 10 MINUTES ↲

150 g (5 oz) cabbage, shredded
200 g (7 oz) green beans, trimmed
2 carrots, sliced
2 potatoes, sliced
100 g (3½ oz) bean sprouts

2 hard-boiled eggs, peeled and quartered
2 tablespoons fried Asian shallots
PEANUT SAUCE:
50 ml (2 fl oz) groundnut oil
200 g (7 oz) peanuts

2 garlic cloves, chopped
4 shallots, chopped
½ teaspoon sambal oelek
1 tablespoon kecap manis
1 tablespoon tamarind concentrate (purée)

1	Steam or boil all the vegetables apart from the fried Asian shallots until tender.	2	For the sauce, heat the oil in a wok and fry the peanuts until golden. Remove with a slotted spoon and drain. Set aside 1 tablespoon of oil.
3	Put the peanuts into a food-processor and whiz into a powder. Pound the garlic and shallots to a paste using a small pestle and mortar.	4	Heat the reserved oil in the wok, add the garlic shallot mixture and cook until golden. ➢

| 5 | Add the peanuts, sambal oelek, kecap manis, tamarind concentrate and 500 ml (17 fl oz) water and cook, stirring occasionally, until the sauce boils and thickens. | **VARIATION**
❊
Use any vegetables for this recipe – try mangetout, cauliflower, sweet potato and broccoli.

SERVING SUGGESTION
❊
This is a great salad to make ahead of time and serve at barbecues. |

6	Serve the vegetables and egg with the peanut sauce and fried Asian shallots.	**SERVING SUGGESTION** ❋ You can also serve some fried tempeh or tofu with the sauce.
TIP ❋ This recipe makes quite a lot of peanut sauce, so store in an airtight container in the fridge and serve with barbecued chicken wings.		**SERVING SUGGESTION** ❋ Serve the gado gado with fried cassava crisps which are available from Asian food stores.

PICKLED VEGETABLE SALAD

→ MAKES 1 LITRE/ 1¾ PINTS • PREPARATION: 50 MINUTES + 8 HOURS PICKLING • COOKING: NIL ←

2 carrots
1 large daikon (white radish)
200 g (7 oz) bean sprouts
1 cucumber

1 red chilli
2 tablespoons sea salt
4 fl oz (125 ml) water
250 ml (8 fl oz) rice vinegar

2 tablespoons caster sugar
3 tablespoon fresh mint leaves
3 tablespoons fresh Vietnamese mint leaves

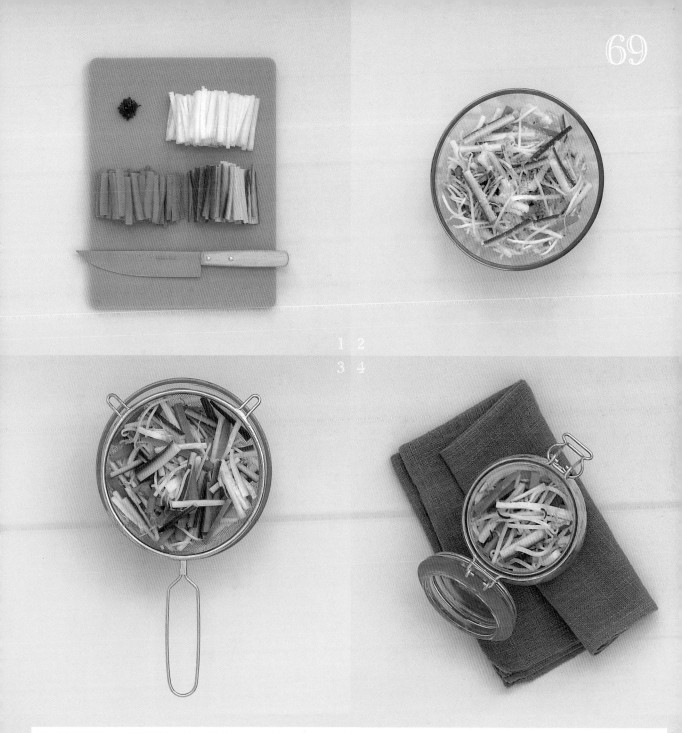

1	Peel and cut the vegetables into thick batons. Chop the chilli finely.	2	Put the vegetables into a non-metallic dish and sprinkle with the salt.
3	Leave the vegetables to stand for 30 minutes, then rinse thoroughly.	4	Pack the vegetables into a vacuum-tight jar. ➤

5	Whisk the measured water, rice vinegar and sugar together and pour over the vegetables.	**TIP** ⁂ Be sure to use a sterilized jar with an airtight lid.
	TIP ⁂ Most Vietnamese meals are served with some of these pickles on the side.	**VARIATION** ⁂ You can vary the vegetables you use or you can cut the vegetables into decorative shapes.

6	Seal and allow to stand overnight. Serve with mint and Vietnamese mint tossed through.	**VARIATION** ❈ If you cannot find Vietnamese mint leaves, use ordinary mint instead.
TIP ❈ Before chopping the red chilli, remove the seeds, if you prefer.		**TIP** ❈ Wash your hands thoroughly after preparing chillies as the volatile oils in them can cause irritation.

STEAMED TOFU WITH GINGER

❖ SERVES 4 · PREPARATION: 10 MINUTES · COOKING: 10 MINUTES ❖

300 g (1 lb) silken firm tofu
1 tablespoon finely shredded fresh ginger
2 tablespoons Shaoxing rice wine

2 tablespoons light soy sauce
1 teaspoon caster sugar
3 spring onions, sliced

1 large red chilli, seeded and thinly sliced
2 tablespoons fried Asian shallots
½ teaspoon white pepper

1	Cut the tofu into 4 large blocks. Place on a large shallow plate and sprinkle with half the shredded ginger.	2	Put the rice wine, soy sauce and sugar in a bowl and mix to combine, then pour half over the tofu.
3	Put the plate into a large bamboo steamer over a wok of simmering water. Cover and cook for 10 minutes.	4	Pour over the remaining sauce and serve with the rest of the ginger, the spring onions, chilli, fried shallots and pepper.

NOODLES WITH VEGETABLES

❧ **SERVES 4** • PREPARATION: 15 MINUTES • COOKING: 10 MINUTES ❧

250 g (8 oz) dried egg noodles
1 tablespoon vegetable oil
1 teaspoon sesame oil
300 g (10 oz) firm tofu, cut into strips

1 red pepper, sliced
1 carrot, sliced
1 courgette, sliced
200 g (7 oz) mangetout

200 g (7 oz) broccoli, cut into florets
3 tablespoons kecap manis
2 teaspoons sambal oelek

1	Cook the noodles in a pan of boiling water until just tender. Drain well.	2	Heat the oils in a wok, add the tofu and stir-fry over a high heat until golden.
3	Add the vegetables and stir-fry for 3 minutes. Combine the kecap manis and sambal oelek. Add the noodles and kecap manis mixture to the wok and fry until the noodles are coated.	4	Divide the noodles and vegetables among 4 serving bowls and serve immediately.

SPINACH & BEAN SALAD

SERVES 4 • PREPARATION: 15 MINUTES + 15 MINUTES SOAKING • COOKING: 15 MINUTES

10 g (½ oz) wakame (seaweed)
200 g (7 oz) green beans, trimmed
300 g (10 oz) baby spinach

DRESSING:
2 tablespoons sesame seeds, toasted
1 egg yolk
3 tablespoons white miso

2 tablespoons sake
½ tablespoon caster sugar
1 tablespoon mirin

1	Soak the wakame in luke-warm water for 15 minutes. Drain well.	2	Steam the beans and spinach until tender, then rinse and cut in half.	3	For the dressing, lightly grind the sesame seeds using a mortar and pestle.
4	Transfer half the sesame seeds to a bowl, stir in the remaining ingredients and whisk to combine.	5	Put the wakame on a plate and top with the spinach and beans.	6	Drizzle with the dressing and serve sprinkled with the remaining sesame seeds.

STIR-FRIED MIXED VEGETABLES

≫ **SERVES 4** • PREPARATION: 15 MINUTES • COOKING: 15 MINUTES ≪

1 tablespoon vegetable oil
1 onion, thinly sliced
2 garlic cloves, chopped
200 g (7 oz) asparagus, cut into
4-cm (1½-in) pieces

200 g (7 oz) sprouting broccoli, roughly
chopped
200 g (7 oz) mangetout
300 g (10 oz) Chinese cabbage, roughly
chopped

125 ml (4 fl oz) water
3 tablespoons Shaoxing rice wine
1 tablespoon light soy sauce
1 tablespoon cornflour

1 2
3 4

1	Heat the oil in a wok, add the onion and garlic and stir-fry for 3 minutes, or until the onion is soft.	2	Add the vegetables and the measured water and stir-fry until soft.
3	Whisk together the rice wine, soy sauce and the cornflour.	4	Add to the vegetables and cook, stirring, until the sauce boils and thickens. Serve.

ASIAN GREENS

※ SERVES 4 • PREPARATION: 5 MINUTES • COOKING: 9 MINUTES ※

1 tablespoon sesame seeds
2 bunches pak choi
2 tablespoons oyster sauce
1 teaspoon sesame oil

1	Toast the sesame seeds in a wok until golden.	2	Wash the pak choi and cut into quarters.
3	Arrange the pak choi evenly over the base of a bamboo steamer and steam in a wok over simmering water for 3–5 minutes until tender.	4	Drizzle with the oyster sauce and sesame oil and sprinkle with the sesame seeds before serving.

DESSERTS

FRUIT DISHES

RICE DISHES

CREAM

WATERMELON & LYCHEE ICE

❖ **SERVES 4–6** • PREPARATION: 20 MINUTES + 8 HOURS FREEZING • COOKING: 2 MINUTES ❖

575 g (18 fl oz) can lychees in natural juice
500 g (1 lb) watermelon, deseeded and
chopped

2 tablespoons grated fresh ginger
75 g (3 oz) caster sugar
50 ml (2 fl oz) lime juice

1 2
3 4

1	Drain the lychees and retain 250 ml (8 fl oz) of the juice.	2	Put the lychees and watermelon into a food-processor and process until puréed.	
3	Strain through a fine sieve, pressing down on any pulp with a back of a metal spoon to remove as much juice as possible. Discard the pulp.	4	Heat the reserved juice, ginger, sugar and lime juice until the sugar dissolves, then bring to the boil. Stand for 10 minutes. Strain, add to the purée and cool.	➤

5	Pour the mixture into a shallow metal baking tray or bowl and put in the freezer. Allow the mixture to start forming an icy edge, which takes about 2 hours. Using a fork, gently mix and mash the ice mixture. Do this every 1–2 hours until you get a nice slushy effect, then freeze completely. This may take overnight

VARIATION
❈

Substitute mango for the watermelon and add some fresh mint or rose water to the recipe.

6	Serve the ice in small dishes.	**SERVING SUGGESTION** ❈ This ice makes a delicious palate cleanser, served between courses at a dinner party.
TIP ❈ The larger the metal tray you use the quicker the liquid will freeze.		**VARIATION** ❈ Add a little vodka or tequila, blend and serve as a refreshing summer cocktail.

DEEP-FRIED BANANAS

❧ SERVES 4 • COOKING: 15 MINUTES • PREPARATION: 15 MINUTES ❧

250 g (8 oz) plain flour
50 g (2 oz) caster sugar, plus extra for
sprinkling
1 egg, lightly beaten

500 ml (17 fl oz) soda water
4 bananas
500 ml (17 fl oz) groundnut oil
ice cream, to serve

1	Put the flour and sugar in a bowl and make a well in the centre.	2	Mix the egg and soda water together, then pour into the centre of the bowl and mix to form a smooth batter.	
3	Cut the bananas in half lengthways then in half across the width.	4	Dip the bananas into the batter, allowing any excess to drain off.	➤

5	Heat the oil in a large wok and deep-fry the bananas until golden. Drain on kitchen paper.	**TIP** ❋ If you don't have a large wok, use a deep saucepan to deep-fry the bananas in step 5.
VARIATION ❋ Add ½ teaspoon each of ground cinnamon and cardamon to the batter.		**SERVING SUGGESTION** ❋ For a typically Asian note, add some toasted sesame seeds to the batter.

6	Sprinkle with sugar and serve with ice cream.	VARIATION ❈ Substitute thinly sliced apple for the bananas.
	TIP ❈ Try to use ripe bananas and cook them just before serving so they are nice and crisp.	SERVING SUGGESTION ❈ Make a caramel sauce and pour this over the bananas at the end.

BLACK STICKY RICE

⇥ SERVES 4 • PREPARATION: 10 MINUTES + 8 HOURS SOAKING • COOKING: 30 MINUTES ⇤

400 g (13 oz) black glutinous rice
1 litre (1¾ pints) water
500 ml (17 fl oz) coconut milk
50 g (2 oz) grated palm sugar

125 ml (4 fl oz) coconut milk, to serve
fresh mango, to serve

1	Put the rice into a bowl, cover with cold water and leave to stand for 8 hours.	2	Bring the rice and the measured water to the boil, then lower the heat and simmer for 20 minutes. Drain well.
3	Put the coconut milk and sugar into another pan and stir until the sugar has dissolved. Add the rice and cook for 10 minutes until hot.	4	Cover and set aside until ready to serve. When ready, drizzle the coconut milk over the top and serve with half a mango per person.

STICKY RICE

⇒ SERVES 4 • PREPARATION: 5 MINUTES + 8 HOURS SOAKING • COOKING: 20 MINUTES ⇐

400 g (13 oz) white sticky rice
250 ml (8 fl oz) coconut milk
50 g (2 oz) white granulated sugar
fresh fruit of your choice, to serve

1	Soak the rice in a bowl of cold water overnight. Rinse and drain well.	2	Put the rice in a steamer lined with baking paper pierced with holes.	3	Put the steamer into a wok over simmering water, cover and cook for 20 minutes.
4	Transfer the rice to a bowl, add the coconut milk and sugar and mix well.	5	Cover and set aside until the rice has absorbed the coconut milk.	6	Serve the sticky rice with your choice of fruit.

CASHEW STAR ANISE BRÛLÉE

❧ SERVES 6 • PREPARATION: 25 MINUTES + 4 HOURS CHILLING • COOKING: 30 MINUTES ❧

250 g (8 oz) roasted unsalted cashews
500 ml (17 fl oz) milk
750 ml (1¼ pints) double cream
3 star anise, broken and bruised

250 g (8 oz) caster sugar
6 egg yolks
50 g (2 oz) caster sugar, for the brulée

1 2
3 4

1	Preheat the oven to 160°C (325°F), Gas Mark 3. Put the cashews in a food processor and process to a smooth paste.	2	Heat the milk, cream, cashews, star anise and 175 g (6 oz) of the sugar to boiling point. Set aside for 10 minutes. Strain the cream mixture.	
3	Beat the egg yolks and remaining sugar together in a bowl until thick and pale. Whisk the infused milk into the egg mixture.	4	Divide the mixture among 6 x 250 ml (8 fl oz) capacity heatproof ramekins and put into a bain-marie.	➤

| 5 | Bake for 30 minutes, or until set. Cool to room temperature, then chill for 4 hours. When ready to serve, sprinkle the top with the 50 g (2 oz) sugar and use a cook's blowtorch to caramelize the sugar. | **TIP**
If you don't have a blowtorch you can cook the brûlee under a hot grill until the sugar caramelizes. |

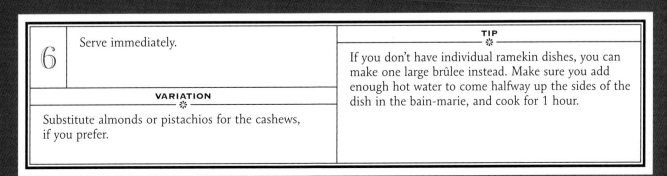

6	Serve immediately.	**TIP** ❊
		If you don't have individual ramekin dishes, you can make one large brûlee instead. Make sure you add enough hot water to come halfway up the sides of the dish in the bain-marie, and cook for 1 hour.
	VARIATION ❊	
	Substitute almonds or pistachios for the cashews, if you prefer.	

LIME & GINGER TART

⇝ SERVES 6–8 • PREPARATION: 30 MINUTES + 20 MINUTES CHILLING • COOKING: 1¼ HOURS ⇜

250 g (8 oz) plain flour
125 g (4 oz) butter, chopped
2 tablespoons caster sugar
1 egg, lightly beaten

FILLING:
2 eggs
3 egg yolks
125 g (4 oz) caster sugar
175 ml (6 fl oz) lime juice

2 tablespoons lime peel
100 ml (3½ fl oz) double cream
2 tablespoons chopped stem ginger
125 ml (4 fl oz) lime or ginger marmalade

1	Preheat the oven to 180°C (350°F), Gas Mark 4. Put the flour in a bowl and rub in the butter.	2	Stir in the sugar, egg and 3–4 tablespoons chilled water until the mixture forms a soft dough.	
				3 Roll out the dough and use to fit a 24-cm (9½-in) tart tin. Prick the base with a fork. Chill for 20 minutes.
4	Blind bake the pastry for 20 minutes. Uncover and bake for 10 minutes.	5	Combine all the filling ingredients, except for the marmalade.	6 Pour into the case and bake (see tip) for 35–45 minutes. Cool. ➤

7	Put the marmalade in a pan and stir over a low heat until the marmalade melts.

VARIATION

Use orange marmalade on top instead of the lime or ginger marmalade, if you prefer.

TIP

Before baking the filled tart (see step 6), be sure to lower the oven temperature to 160°C (325°F), Gas Mark 3.

8	Pour over the top of the tart and leave to cool. Serve cut into wedges.	**SERVING SUGGESTION** ❈ This tart is delicious served either warm or cold with crème fraîche or cream. Store in an airtight container in the fridge after slicing.

VARIATIONS
❈

For a stronger ginger flavour add 1 teaspoon of ground ginger to the egg mixture and use crystallized ginger instead of stem ginger.

KAFFIR LIME CRÈME CARAMEL

❧ SERVES 4 • PREPARATION: 30 MINUTES + 4 HOURS CHILLING • COOKING: 50 MINUTES ❧

6 kaffir lime leaves
125 g (4 oz) white granulated sugar
250 ml (8 fl oz) milk

250 ml (8 fl oz) coconut milk
125 g (4 oz) caster sugar
4 eggs, lightly beaten

1 2
3 4

1	Preheat the oven to 160°C (325°F), Gas Mark 3. Shred the lime leaves finely.	2	Gently heat the granulated sugar in a pan until it dissolves. Increase the heat and cook until it caramelizes. Divide among 4 ramekins.	
3	Heat the milk, coconut milk and shredded lime leaves until boiling point. Remove from the heat and leave for 15 minutes. Strain.	4	Whisk the caster sugar and eggs together in a bowl to combine.	➤

| 5 | Add the milk and divide the mixture among the ramekins. Put the ramekins in a bain-marie and add enough water to come halfway up the side of the dishes. Bake for 40 minutes, or until set | **TIP** ❋

Make sure you allow the desserts to chill, preferably overnight, otherwise it may be difficult to get them out of the moulds. |

6	Chill for 4 hours before inverting onto serving plates.	**TIP** ※ Be sure to use 250 ml (8 fl oz) capacity heatproof ramekin dishes.
TIP ※ If you prefer to have a stronger kaffir lime flavour, use all milk rather than coconut milk for this recipe.		**VARIATION** ※ Use a 20-cm (8-in) dish to make one large crème caramel, if you prefer, and cook for 1 hour.

SAGO PUDDING

❧ **SERVES 4** • PREPARATION: 5 MINUTES • COOKING: 20 MINUTES + 30 MINUTES STANDING ❧

100 g (3½ oz) sago
500 ml (17 fl oz) water
400 ml (13 fl oz) coconut cream
50 g (2 oz) grated palm sugar

1 2
3 4

1	Put the sago and the measured water into a pan, bring to the boil and cook over a high heat for 10 minutes.	2	Turn off the heat, cover and leave to stand for 30 minutes, or until the sago has become thick and transparent.
3	Add the coconut cream and sugar.	4	Stir over a medium heat for 10 minutes, or until the sago thickens. Serve immediately.

GREEN TEA PANNA COTTA

❧ **SERVES 6** • PREPARATION: 25 MINUTES + 4 HOURS CHILLING • COOKING: 5 MINUTES ❧

1 tablespoon Japanese green tea powder
250 ml (8 fl oz) milk
500 ml (17 fl oz) double cream

125 g (4 oz) caster sugar
1½ tablespoons powdered gelatine
vegetable oil, for oiling

1	Blend the green tea powder with a little milk in order to dissolve. Stir in the remaining milk.	2	Heat the tea, milk, cream and sugar until the sugar dissolves, then heat to boiling point. Set aside.	3	Blend the gelatine with a little warm water until soft. Whisk into the milk mixture until it dissolves.
4	Lightly oil 6 x 125 ml (4 fl oz) moulds or ramekins.	5	Divide the mixture among the moulds and chill for 4 hours, or until set.	6	Rub the outside of the moulds with a damp cloth and invert onto plates.

APPENDICES

GLOSSARY

MENUS

TABLE OF CONTENTS

INDEX OF RECIPES

GENERAL INDEX

ACKNOWLEDGEMENTS

GLOSSARY

ASIAN SHALLOTS
These are smaller than French shallots and come in small purplish bunches that resemble long garlic cloves. French shallots or red onions may be used as a substitute. Shallots are used in curry pastes, soups and salads. You can deep-fry them and add them to salads, or use as a garnish. Deep-fried shallots can be purchased in jars in Asian food stores.

BAMBOO SHOOTS
The young cone-shaped shoots of the bamboo plant are usually sold in cans and have more flavour than their pre-sliced counterparts. Rinse under cold running water before using.

BLACK GLUTINOUS ('STICKY') RICE
Black sticky rice is only used to make desserts, and, like white sticky rice, it needs to be soaked in cold water overnight before cooking.

BONITO FLAKES
These are made from dried skipjack tuna and are much used in Japanese cooking. The bonito is shaved in fine slivers, which are sprinkled over dishes just before serving to add a mild fish flavour.

COCONUT MILK/CREAM
Coconut cream is thicker than coconut milk and will solidify at the top of the can. It is usually used to cook curry paste in instead of oil. If you want to use coconut cream, do not shake the can before opening – you can then remove the thick cream with a spoon. Alternatively, you can buy cartons of coconut cream in most supermarkets. Use coconut milk in curries or stir-fries.

CHILLIES
Large red chillies – These are widely used in Thai cooking to add colour. They are mild and can be tolerated by most palates if you remove the seeds.
Small red – Also known as bird's eye chillies, these are fiery. The heat is in the seed and membrane. For a spicy dish, chop the flesh and include the seeds; for a milder dish, halve the chilli, and for a very mild dish leave them whole and discard before serving. Always use rubber gloves when preparing chillies.
Dried large red – These are not so spicy because the seeds have been removed. To use, soak them in hot water for 10 minutes, then drain and chop. Dried chillies are used to make red curry pastes.

Small green – These chillies are milder than small red chillies and can be used to make green curry paste. They are not as hot as large green chillies.
Large green – These are hotter than large red chillies. Use them in green curry paste if you like it really spicy.

CHILLI JAM
This is a thick sweet chilli paste sold in Asian food stores. It is used in Thai cooking and is an essential ingredient in any dish that uses chilli and basil.

CORIANDER
Also known as cilantro or Chinese parsley, this is widely used in Thai and Chinese cooking. The root is often used in making curry pastes. Coriander has a delicious peppery flavour. Store wrapped in damp kitchen paper in an airtight container or plastic bag.

DASHI
This is an essential ingredient in Japanese cooking and is known as the basic stock. You can buy dashi granules and just add water to make dashi stock or you can make your own by simmering dried bonito flakes and seaweed in water before straining the liquid.

DRIED CHINESE (SHIITAKE) MUSHROOMS
These mushrooms vary in price and quality. To reconstitute, cover with boiling water and leave to stand for 10 minutes. Remove the stems and discard, then finely shred the caps. The soaking liquid may be used to add flavour to soups and sauces.

DRIED MUNG BEAN VERMICELLI
Also called glass noodles, these are clear thread-like noodles that are used in salads and spring rolls. Vermicelli need to be soaked in water before using.

DRIED RICE NOODLES
These long thin white noodles are best known for their use in Pad Thai. Soak them in cold water for 15 minutes; this way they will not overcook and break up when you add them to the wok.

DRIED SHRIMP
Tiny shrimp that have been dried in the sun, these are widely used in Asian cooking to add a mild shrimp flavour to dishes. They can be fried in oil or added as they are to salads or stir-fries.

FISH SAUCE

This is made from fermented, salted anchovies and is widely used in Thai and Vietnamese cooking instead of salt. The Thais call it nam pla and the Vietnamese nuoc man. Its level of saltiness will vary depending on the brand, so it is a good idea to taste before using or add sparingly.

FRESH RICE NOODLES

These flat rice noodles are available from Asian food stores. They are sold at room temperature and are either sold pre-sliced or in blocks that need to be cut into strips before using. Avoid refrigerating them if you can, as this tends to make them break up. Try to buy them on the day you need them.

GALANGAL

This looks like a dark pink gnarled ginger but its flesh is firmer and woodier than root ginger and its flavour is much more concentrated. To use, peel and pound using a mortar and pestle. You can add galangal slices to soups, but it is best known for its use in Tom Kai Gai. Use root ginger if you cannot find galangal.

GINGER

Fresh ginger is widely used in Asian cooking; its peppery flavour intensifies with age. Peel before using, then grate and add to stir-fries or curries, or cut into thin slices and add to soups or stews.

GREEN PAPAYA

This is an unripe papaya used in salads. To use, peel and remove the seeds then grate or shred finely.

GREEN TEA NOODLES

These are buckwheat noodles that have had green tea powder added.

GREEN TEA POWDER

This is used in Japanese desserts. Use it sparingly as it is quite expensive. It needs to be blended with a little milk or water before using.

GYOZA WRAPPERS

White square wheat flour wrappers used to make Japanese dumplings of the same name, these are available in the refrigerator section of Asian food stores.

HOISIN

Probably best known as the sauce served on Peking duck pancakes, hoisin sauce is made from salted yellow beans, sugar, vinegar, sesame oil and five spice powder. It is delicious on its own as a dipping sauce for Vietnamese rice paper rolls or when added to marinades and sauces.

JAPANESE CURRY

This paste-like curry is sold in boxes in Asian food stores and comes in a variety of temperatures. Purchase according to your palate.

JAPANESE MAYONNAISE

This thick squeezable mayonnaise is prized by the Japanese as a condiment and is also used as a sushi flavouring. It is sold in jars in Asian food stores.

JASMINE RICE

This is a fragrant long-grain rice that is highly prized in Thai cooking. It is steamed and served at all meals. Rinse the rice before using. Basmati rice has a totally different flavour and it not really considered to be a substitute.

KAFFIR LIME LEAVES

These are fragrant, glossy, double leaves that give Thai curries their distinctive taste. To use, remove the tough middle stem, tear the leaves and add to soups and curries, or finely shred them in salads and stir-fries. Fresh leaves can be frozen. Dried leaves can be used instead, but they don't have the wonderful pungent lime flavour of fresh kaffir lime leaves.

KECAP MANIS

This is a thick sweet soy sauce that is used in stir-fries, dipping sauces, dressings and marinades. Indonesian kecap manis comes in three types: sweet (red label); mild sweet (yellow label) and salty (green label).

LEMONGRASS

A long strappy grass-like herb that is widely used in Thai and Vietnamese cooking. The outer layers are tough and need to be peeled off. The firm white portion is finely chopped or pounded and used in curries, stir-fries or marinades, while the grassy tops can be used in teas.

LUP CHEONG

This is a sweet Chinese sausage or salami.

MIRIN

This is a very sweet rice wine that is used only for cooking and not drinking. It adds sweetness to dishes and gives grilled basted foods such as Yakitori a glossy finish. If you can't find mirin you can sweeten sake with sugar. Add 1 teaspoon of sugar to 1 tablespoon of sake.

MISO

This is fermented soybean paste and is widely used in Japanese cuisine. As a rule, the lighter the colour, the milder the flavour, and the darker the colour, the richer and more salty the flavour. Light miso is more widely used in summer and dark miso is used in winter.

NORI

These are flat square sheets of seaweed that are used to make sushi. You can purchase roasted or unroasted, but the roasted sheets have more flavour.

OYSTER SAUCE

A thick dark sauce much used in Cantonese stir-fries and marinades. It is made from oyster extract, sugar, salt, caramel and flour. Vegetarians can use mushroom oyster sauce, which is less thick.

PALM SUGAR

This is a type of sugar made from the sap of the trunk of the coconut or sugar palm. It is sold in round blocks and comes in two colours: blond or dark brown. Use a sharp knife to shave the firmer block or grate the softer ones. If you can't buy palm sugar use brown sugar instead.

PANKO BREADCRUMBS

Japanese breadcrumbs, these coarse textured breadcrumbs are sold in bags in Asian food stores and are an essential ingredient in Tonkatsu. If you can't find them you can make your own by toasting and roughly crushing one day-old bread.

PICKLED GINGER

This is sliced ginger that has been pickled in vinegar and often dyed to give a pink blush, though the flavour is the same in the uncoloured ones. Served with both sushi and sashimi, pickled ginger is used widely as a condiment in Japan.

RED CURRY PASTE

This is made from dried red chillies that have been pounded in a mortar and pestle with Asian shallots and spices. It is not as hot as green curry paste, but it is a good idea to test for heat before using as brands will vary. Asian brands are usually a little spicier.

RICE PAPER ROUNDS

These dried discs are used to make Vietnamese rice paper rolls. To use, soak in lukewarm water. They come in a variety of sizes; larger are easier to roll.

RICE VINEGAR

Chinese rice vinegar is made from fermented rice. It comes in a variety of colours and each colour has its specific use. Clear vinegar is used for pickles and if you can't find it you can use cider vinegar instead. Red vinegar is used as a dipping sauce for dumplings and black vinegar is used in braises.

SAGO

Small pearls of sago are made from the root of the cassava plant. Cooked in water until it becomes translucent it can then be flavoured with coconut milk, mango or other fruits. It is served either warm or cold as a dessert.

SAKE

This is rice wine that is widely used in Japanese cooking as a tenderizer. It moderates the saltiness of a dish and removes the strong fishy flavours. Boil sake if you wish to remove the alcohol content.

SALTED BLACK BEANS

Probably best known as the ingredient used in beef and black bean sauce, these beans are pressed into a block and need to be separated before adding to dishes. If you can't find them then use tinned black beans, but don't confuse these with the pre-made black bean sauce.

SHAOXING

This is the most renowned Chinese rice wine. It is an amber-coloured liquid widely used in braises, soups and sauces.

SHRIMP PASTE

Also known as gapi, this pungent paste is used to add a rich seafood flavour to Asian dishes. It should be roasted or fried in oil before adding to dishes. Store in an airtight container in the freezer.

SOBA NOODLES

Traditionally these stone-grey coloured noodles were made from buckwheat, but these days a lot of brands are a combinaton of buckwheat and wheat. Allow about 100 g (3½ oz) of dried noodles per person and be careful not to overcook them.

SOY SAUCE

Most people are not aware that there are two types of soy sauce – light and dark. Light soy sauce is used in stir-fries, marinades and dressings, while dark is used in stews and stocks.

SPRING ONION PANCAKES

These are round wheat flour pancakes that are used for Peking duck. They are available in the freezer section of Asian food stores or are sometimes available where you purchase your duck.

STAR ANISE

This star-shaped spice is an integral flavouring in Chinese cooking. Star anise is widely used in stocks, soups and braises, and is an essential ingredient in five-spice powder.

SUSHI RICE

This is a short-grain rice used for making sushi as it has a higher starch content, which means it sticks together once cooked. Rinse thoroughly under cold running water before using.

SWEET CHILLI SAUCE

This is used as a condiment for fried chicken in Thailand. Sweet chilli sauce will vary in intensity and sweetness depending on the brand. It is also great in dressings and marinades, but thin it with a little water if it is too thick.

TAMARIND

This comes in two forms: a solid block that contains both the pulp and seeds and the concentrate or purée. It needs to be prepared before use. The pulp is first broken apart and then covered in boiling water to soften. The pulp and seeds are then strained off to leave the sour liquid. Tamarind is widely used in Thai cooking to add a pleasing sourness to soups and curries.

THAI BASIL (HORAPA)

The purple-tinged stem and finer, more pointed, leaves are the easiest way to differentiate Thai basil from Greek basil. Thai basil has a much stronger anise flavour than its Mediterranean cousin.

TOFU

Also known as beancurd, tofu comes in a variety of textures. Silken, which is mainly used in desserts, silken firm, which is suitable for soups, and firm, which is best for stir-fries and curries. You can also purchase deep-fried tofu, which is delicious added to soups, stir-fries and curries where it acts like a sponge to soak up the flavour of the sauce.

UDON NOODLES

These are Japanese wheat noodles that are available pre-cooked or dried in supermarkets. These thick worm-like noodles can be used in soups, stir-fries and salads.

VIETNAMESE MINT

Also known as laksa leaf, this leaf is widely used in Vietnamese cooking – as the name would imply. Its elongated pointed leaf has a strong spicy mint flavour. If you can't find it use spearmint instead.

WAKAME

This is a type of dried seaweed and is valued for its flavour and texture. It is widely used in soups (namely miso) and salads, where is goes well with vinegared dressings.

WASABI

This is Japanese horseradish. It is sold either in a tube as a paste or in a powder form that needs to have water added to form a paste. Its heat will clear the sinuses, so use sparingly if you don't like hot spicy stuff.

WATER CHESTNUTS

Packed in tins, water chestnuts are widely available in supermarkets. Rinse well before using.

WHITE OR SHIRO MISO

A mild sweet miso that is used in soups and is also delicious in dressings.

WHITE GLUTINOUS ('STICKY') RICE

This is mainly eaten in the north of Thailand where it is always served as an accompaniment to Som Tam (green papaya salad). It can be served either as a sweet or savoury rice and needs to be soaked in cold water overnight before cooking to soften the grain.

WONTON WRAPPERS

These square or round yellow wrappers are used for wontons and dim sum. They are available in the refrigerated or freezer section of your supermarket or Asian food stores.

YELLOW ROCK SUGAR

Looking more like a crystal than sugar, this amber-coloured sugar is used in Chinese stocks and stews to add a gloss to the finished dish.

MENUS

JAPANESE

1
Miso soup.. 07
Edamame... 12
Gyoza 13
California rolls................................. 14
Sashimi 17

2
Yaki soba 22
Sesame beef salad 25
Pork tonkatsu.................................. 29
Japanese beef curry 32

3
Spicy fried chicken 33
Chilli chicken ramen....................... 34
Teriyaki chicken 43
Yakitori chicken 45

4
Fish with miso 58
Chirashi sushi................................. 61
Temaki sushi 62

5
Agedashi tofu 63
Vegetable tempura 64
Spinach & bean salad...................... 72

6
Lime & ginger tart 80
Green tea panna cotta 83

CHINESE

1
Chicken & corn soup 06
Dim sum 11
Prawn toast...................................... 16

2
Sung choi bau 20
Char sui pork 24

3
Chicken with cashews...................... 42
Peking duck..................................... 46
Marinated chicken wings 47
Crispy spiced duck.......................... 48

4
Asian oysters 51
Steamed fish with ginger 55
Scallops & mangetout 56
Fried rice with prawns..................... 60

5
Chinese vegetable omelette 67
Steamed tofu with ginger................. 70
Stir-fried mixed vegetables.............. 73
Asian greens 74

6
Watermelon & lychee ice 75
Cashew star anise brûlée 79
Sago pudding................................... 82

VIETNAMESE

1	Pho bo .... 08 Goi cuon .... 09 Nems 10	2	Shaking beef .... 23 Bun cha .... 26 Bo bun 28
3	Vietnamese chicken curry .... 39 Vietnamese chicken salad 44	4	Salt & pepper squid .... 53 Clay pot salmon 57
5	Pickled vegetable salad 69	6	Black sticky rice 77

THAI

1	Tom yum goong .... 04 Tom kai gai .... 05 Fish cakes 15	2	Larb moo .... 19 Beef in black bean sauce .... 21 Masaman beef 30
3	Chicken pad Thai .... 35 Duck & pineapple curry .... 36 Chicken green curry .... 38 Stir-fried chicken .... 40 Chicken with lemongrass 41	4	Sweet chilli squid salad .... 50 Mussels with lemongrass .... 52 Salt & pepper squid .... 53 Seafood red curry 54
5	Vegetable green curry .... 65 Steamed tofu with ginger 70	6	Black sticky rice .... 77 Sticky rice .... 78 Kaffir lime crème caramel 81

INDONESIAN

1	Chicken satay 18	2	Babi ketjap .... 27 Beef rendang 31
3	Nasi goreng 49	4	Seafood noodles 59
5	Satay pumpkin curry .... 66 Gado gado .... 68 Noodles with vegetables 71	6	Deep-fried bananas .... 76 Black sticky rice 77

TABLE OF CONTENTS

1
STARTERS

SOUPS

SNACKS

APPETIZERS

2
MEAT

STIR-FRIES

GRILLS & ROASTS

CLASSICS

CURRIES

3

POULTRY

NOODLE DISHES

COCONUT MILK DISHES

STIR-FRIES

CLASSICS

4

SEAFOOD

QUICK & EASY DISHES

SIMPLE MAIN DISHES

RICE & NOODLE DISHES

SUSHI

5

VEGETABLES

6

DESSERTS

INDEX OF RECIPES

Note: This index is organized by recipe number.

GENERAL INDEX

Note: This index is organized by recipe number.

ACKNOWLEDGEMENTS

Writing, photographing and publishing a cookbook is by no means a one-woman show.
I would like to thank the following essential hardworking members of this team for their
commitment to this beautiful book. At Marabout, Jennifer Joly for managing the book through
its stages and being a pleasure to deal with, and Emmanuel for the original design and the
gorgeous colour scheme. Catie Ziller, for pulling it together in a heavily pregnant state.
Clive Bozzard-Hill, the cleverest crossword doer I've ever met and oh yeah I'd better mention
how fantastic he is at photography and arranging ingredients. His stunning wife, Jane Bozzard-
Hill, the book's designer, for doing such a great job with the layout of so many photos.

To Zoe and Lucie for the big smiles they brought home from school each day and for letting
me take over their playroom with my props. My wonderful group of assistants who helped me
in the kitchen: Sarah Delulio, Rob Allison and Belinda Altenroxel. Also to Byron, Sasha,
Caitlin and Elice for making my stay in their family home an absolute hoot, thanks for
reacquainting me with my inner teenager.

My righthand woman, Tracey Gordon, who makes my job an absolute joy, it was so special to
be back in the hot seat with you chef, the fastest chopper/cooker in the West. It was lovely to
work again with my editor Kathy Steer who has the amazing ability to calm me from the
other side of the world with her watchful eye. Annie, my gorgeous girlfriend, for taking
care of all my business stuff while I was o'seas, in between buying and selling a house
and saving people's lives.

Oh and one can't let a cookbook pass by without a mention to my beloved Pridey girl;
if you don't own a dog you will think I'm a freak, but if you do you will know their friendship
is unrivalled. A big thanks to Dave for taking such good care of her while I was in London
shooting this book.

And finally, to my cherished friends and family for being the spine that holds me upright.
Your love and tireless support is valued more than Macquarie Bank shares.

Author: Jody Vassallo
Photographer: Clive Bozzard-Hill
Art Editor: Jane Bozzard-Hill
Project Editor: Kathy Steer
English adaptation: JMS Books llp
Layout: cbdesign